Pentecost 2

Proclamation 3

Aids for Interpreting the Lessons of the Church Year

Pentecost 2

Patrick D. Miller, Jr.

Elizabeth Achtemeier, series editor

Series A

FORTRESS PRESS Philadelphia

Library of Congress Cataloging in Publication Data

Main entry under title:

Proclamation 3.

Consists of 28 volumes in 3 series designated A, B, and C which correspond to the cycles of the three year lectionary. Each series contains 8 basic volumes with the following titles: Advent-Christmas, Epiphany, Lent, Holy Week, Easter, Pentecost 1, Pentecost 2, and Pentecost 3.

1. Bible—Homiletical use. 2. Bible—Liturgical lessons, English. I. Achtemeier, Elizabeth Rice, 1926–

BS534.5.P765 1985 251 84-18756

ISBN 0-8006-4106-X (Series B, Pentecost 1)

2570G86 Printed in the United States of America 1-4123

Contents

Series Foreword

Proclamation 3 is an entirely new aid for preaching from the three-year ecumenical lectionary. In outward appearance this new series is similar to *Proclamation: Aids for Interpreting the Lessons of the Church Year* and *Proclamation 2*. But *Proclamation 3* has a new content as well as a new purpose.

First, there is only one author for each of the twenty-eight volumes of *Proclamation 3*. This means that each author handles both the exegesis and the exposition of the stated texts, thus eliminating the possibility of disparity between scholarly apprehension and homiletical application of the appointed lessons. While every effort was made in *Proclamation: Aids* and in *Proclamation 2* to avoid such disparity, it tended to creep in occasionally. *Proclamation 3* corrects that tendency.

Second, *Proclamation 3* is directed primarily at homiletical interpretation of the stated lessons. We have again assembled the finest biblical scholars and preachers available to write for the series; now, however, they bring their skills to us not primarily as exegetes, but as interpreters of the Word of God. Exegetical material is still presented—sometimes at length—but, most important, here it is also applied; the texts are interpreted and expounded homiletically for the church and society of our day. In this new series scholars become preachers. They no longer stand back from the biblical text and just discuss it objectively. They engage it—as the Word of God for the worshiping community. The reader therefore will not find here the divisions between "exegesis" and "homiletical interpretation" that were marked off in the two earlier series. In *Proclamation 3* the work of the pulpit is the context and goal of all that is written.

There is still some slight diversity between the several lections and calendars of the various denominations. In an effort to overcome such diversity, the North American Committee on a Common Lectionary issued an experimental "consensus lectionary" (*The Common Lectionary*), which is now being tried out in some congregations and which will be further altered at the end of a three-year period. When the final form of that lectionary appears, *Proclamation* will take account of it.

In the meantime, *Proclamation 3* deals with those texts that are used by *most* denominations on any given Sunday. It also continues to use the Lutheran numbering of the Sundays "after Pentecost." But Episcopalians and Roman Catholics will find most of their stated propers dealt with under this numbering.

Each author writes on three lessons for each Sunday, but no one method of combining the appointed lessons has been imposed upon the writers. The texts are sometimes treated separately, sometimes together—according to the author's own understanding of the texts' relationships and messages. The authors interpret the appointed texts as these texts have spoken to them.

Patrick D. Miller, Jr. is Professor of Old Testament Theology at Princeton Theological Seminary, and the Old Testament editor of *Interpretation: A Bible Commentary for Teaching and Preaching*. Educated at Union Theological Seminary in Virginia and Harvard University, he served a pastorate in South Carolina and was then a member of the faculty of Union Theological Seminary in Virginia from 1966 to 1984. A Presbyterian, he is the author of many scholarly articles and an editor for several theological journals.

The Tenth Sunday After Pentecost

Lutheran	Roman Catholic	Episcopal	Pres/UCC/Chr	Meth/COCU
1 Kings 3:5–12	1 Kings 3:5, 7–12	1 Kings 3:5–12	1 Kings 3:5–12	1 Kings 3:5–12
Rom. 8:28–30	Rom. 8:28–30	Rom. 8:26–34	Rom. 8:26–30	Rom. 8:28–30
Matt. 13:44–52	Matt. 13:44–52 or Matt. 13:44–46	Matt. 13:31–33, 44–49a	Matt. 13:44–52	Matt. 13:44–52

OLD TESTAMENT: 1 KINGS 3:5–12

One of the concerns reflected in the Deuteronomistic History (Deuteronomy through Kings) is the development of a theology and practice of leadership in the community that lives under the rule of God. This text, like others (e.g., Deut. 1:9–18; 17:14–20; Josh. 1:6–9; 2 Sam. 8:15; 2 Kings 22—23), contributes to that understanding and serves to shape a notion of the nature of leadership that is derived from and subordinate to the guidance and authority of God. Solomon did not demonstrate such leadership in perfect fashion, but in his words about David and his petitions to God some clues are given that by their consistency with other words of Scripture are of enduring worth as the church calls some—indeed many—to positions of authority and leadership.

Four characteristics mark the kind of rule and authority exemplified in Solomon's prayer and God's response. One of these is contextual. The king's leadership of the people is carried out in the context of *a covenantal relationship with God.* All of the language of Solomon's opening words in v. 6 testifies to the fact that the rule of the people is in the hands of one who is bound to the Lord in a perduring relationship in which both the king and God are committed to each other. The ruler expects in the face of the vicissitudes, mistakes, and sins of human life to be kept and sustained by the love of God, who will not give up the relationship. The ruler seeks in every aspect of governance and personal conduct to manifest fidelity to God. It is this commitment of leader to Lord and Lord to leader that is the ground of all that the king does.

The other characteristics of rule and authority, therefore, flow out of and reflect this covenantal relationship. The ruler is one whose self-understanding is focused on *service.* In each verse of Solomon's prayer he describes himself or David as "thy servant," acknowledging thereby that his rule is derivative from God's rule and carried out in behalf of and in the service of another as indeed a servant carries out the assigned tasks of his or her master. Solomon's reference to himself as "a little child" is a further reflection of this self-understanding of the ruler. Not only does it convey his sense of humility, but it is acknowledgment not so much of a youthful age as of a sense of complete dependence upon God.

The king does not speak of himself as servant of the people, but it is clear that understanding himself as God's servant affects the way in which he understands his relation to the people. That is demonstrated in two ways. One is Solomon's consistent identification of his subjects as "thy people," that is, God's people. The ruler knows that the covenantal relationship, the shared commitment, is not only between king and God but between people and God. The people have their primary definition in the mind of this leader not as "*my* subjects," but as "*your* people," whom the king is to rule and govern as "*your* servant." The nature of Solomon's petition in v. 9 is indicative also of the king's role vis-à-vis the people. His prayer is not for self-enhancement in various ways—as one might have expected (see v. 11)—but for qualities that will enable him to lead or serve God's people. The king describes himself as "thy servant" and "a little child" while understanding the people as "thy people" and a "great people" (vv. 8, 9).

As to the actual nature and content of the leadership exemplified in Solomon's prayer, two things stand out. One is the identification of the rule of the king as a *faithful walking before the Lord.* Here, too, the covenantal relationship is reflected, for this is what is expected of one who lives and acts in covenant with God—faithfulness in following the Lord's way. Such a definition calls to mind the law of the king in Deut. 17:14–20. There the essential responsibility of the king is to have before him at all times a copy of the Mosaic law and to keep all its words and statutes, or as it is otherwise stated, "to learn to fear the Lord" (v. 19). The essential responsibility of the leader of the people is, therefore, obedience to the will of God as discerned from the instruction of God that has been communicated and then handed down within the community of faith. In some sense the ideal king as defined this way is the model Israelite. Faithful walking in the way of the Lord is both the way of exercising leadership as chosen and servant of God and also an example of the way and the responsibility of every other member of the community.

Finally, the theological understanding of leadership of God's people that is embodied in this text centers on the need for *an understanding mind* (literally, "a hearing heart/mind," v. 9), "*a wise and discerning mind*" (v. 12). The knowledge of what is right and best, of what works effectively and for the good of individual and community, the capacity to discern the issues, to distinguish between right and wrong, good and bad, helpful and unhelpful—these are the qualities of leadership sought by Solomon. It is clear from much of the Old Testament, as well as from the human story generally, that such qualities grow out of experience. It is equally clear from *this* story and again from common human experience that such traits are also gifts of God, to be sought and prayed for by those in whose hands the responsibilities of leadership have fallen.

GOSPEL: MATTHEW 13:44–52

These verses conclude one of Jesus' discourses on the kingdom. Like all parables their power to communicate arises out of the use of sharp and pointed images or stories. In the best sense of the term they are illustrations that catch the attention of the hearer and convey a message with vividness that creates a lasting impression and thus a capacity to recall. They remind the contemporary interpreter and preacher of the power and value of images, pictures, and stories in the proclamation of the word, and they offer themselves directly as such for the contemporary act of proclamation.

The appropriate focus of interpretation of these parables (actually similes) is the two comparisons of the kingdom of heaven to a buried treasure and a pearl of great value. Verses 47–50 represent what was probably originally a simple comparison of the kingdom to a net that gathers many fish, good and bad—a comparison that has been extended to a parable on the last judgment analogous to 13:40–41. The final two verses (51–52) are a conclusion to the whole discourse in which the disciples indicate their understanding of Jesus' parables—a critical step forward in their discipleship. In making his final point about disciples of the kingdom, drawing upon both God's instruction in the past (the Old Testament) and his own new interpretation of it, Jesus indirectly addresses the issue raised in the discussion of Solomon's dream—the nature of leadership under God's rule. Here one sees that those who are scholars or teachers of the law (scribes), positions of leadership and honor in the religious community, are disciples in the kingdom of heaven, trained for the kingdom. The rabbi or "great one" is in the kingdom "a little one," "thy servant" (1 Kings 3), who learns to go the way of the Lord.

The heart of the Gospel lessons are two short but powerful and joyous parables in vv. 44–46. They are very short and positive lessons about what it means to be subjects of the kingdom of heaven, those who give themselves over to the rule of God. Both passages sound essentially the same notes. One of these is the inestimable worth of life in the kingdom. The notion of treasure is prominent in Matthew's Gospel (cf. v. 52) and especially as here, a way of conveying what it means to be drawn into, to find (v. 44) the kingdom. One has to think of buried treasure and glittering gems to get a sense of the value of belonging to God's kingdom. Is that something to be sought after earnestly or is it something that one only discovers as a surprise? The two parables leave that question open as they point us in different directions. Where they are agreed, however, and score the crucial point is that *for the kingdom of heaven, it is worth giving up everything else* (compare vv. 44b and 46b). Note that this does not happen on the basis of instruction or obligation to sacrifice everything (though we see that elsewhere in the Gospels). But here Jesus' point is that one who has found the kingdom whether by accident or earnest intention will give anything to belong to it. It is far better than any present possessions, any existing reality, so one will want to "sell all" to attain something even greater. The surrender of everything is a way of speaking of a total commitment to doing God's will because that way leads to a life that is better than any other, one that is characterized by joy (v. 44). A similar word to these parables is sounded in Paul's Epistle to the Philippians, a letter that rings with notes of joy:

> But *whatever gain* I had, *I counted as loss* for the sake of Christ. Indeed *I count everything as loss* because of the surpassing worth of knowing Christ Jesus my Lord. For his sake I have suffered *the loss of all things,* and count them as refuse, in order that I may gain Christ. (Phil. 3:7–8)

EPISTLE: ROMANS 8:28–30

The section of Paul's Letter to the Romans from which these verses are drawn has been called by one interpreter "Paul's most impressive confession of the triumph of God."[1] Verse 28 is criticized by some as reflecting a naive view of existence while others count it one of the most fundamental expressions of the assurance of the gospel in the New Testament.

In a quite specific way Paul's words in this section echo the Gospel lesson in Matthew. In v. 32 the apostle says, "Will he not also give us *all things* with him?" The surrender of everything, the paying of any price in the way of discipleship is for the sake of an even greater future. That future is assured by the triumph of God's grace, a triumph that is anticipated and assured in the death and resurrection of God's own beloved child Jesus Christ. The note of joy that is present in the parable of the discovery of buried treasure is here also, a joy and confidence that is authentic and justifiable whatever the present situation precisely because the future, *our* future, is not determined by our actions or those of others (although it is always affected by such for good or ill). There is no basis for ultimate confidence in our own experience or the deeds or capacities of others. Indeed there one can find the seeds of the deepest pessimism—witness the universal fear of a humanly determined nuclear apocalypse. It is only in the certitude that the world is not simply filled with evil and suffering but indeed is cruciform, stamped with the suffering love of Christ, and theocentric, controlled in its destiny by one who brings life out of death and guides our destiny to that end, continually shaping us in life and death to the image of God's Son. That is the good toward which God is working *in everything*. This is not and was not a romantic view of human existence. Paul may be accused of many things but naiveté about what life was like is not one of them. His own experience bore witness to the suffering that can and probably will come to those who surrender everything for the kingdom (v. 18). Indeed the beautiful words of v. 28, which find their confirmation only in a future beyond our knowing, ring true in the clearest way only in the experience of suffering. A teacher of the New Testament many years ago who was critically injured in a terrible car accident returned to consciousness in a hospital bed and received the message that his wife had been killed. He sent the message back: "Tell my students that Romans 8:28 still holds good." In some sense he was indicating that now he knew the reality of Paul's words and trusted them in a way that he had never been called on to do before.

The conviction of *God's* ultimate triumph for the *good* of those who belong to God's kingdom is restated in v. 29, which describes the Christian pilgrimage in highly theological terms—known beforehand in the mind of God, set to a destiny with Christ, called into the kingdom and a way of holy living, brought into a right relationship with God, and given a glorious future with God. God is the subject of all those verbs. From before our beginning to beyond our end, all is shaped and directed by God for a positive destiny that cannot be described in this world but can be characterized as good and glorified. In this light the words of judgment in the parable of the fish that are sorted out (Matt. 13:47–50) can finally be heard as a piece of good news. Who and what the bad fish are can never be said with much specificity. But those who know their destiny to be directed by the God whose love is revealed in Jesus Christ understand the judgment to be a word about the good that God will work out in everything for those whom God has set for glory.

The Eleventh Sunday After Pentecost

Lutheran	Roman Catholic	Episcopal	Pres/UCC/Chr	Meth/COCU
Isa. 55:1–5	Isa. 55:1–3	Neh. 9:16–20	Isa. 55:1–3	Neh. 9:16–20
Rom. 8:35–39	Rom. 8:35, 37–39	Rom. 8:35–39	Rom. 8:31–39	Rom. 8:31–39
Matt. 14:13–21	Matt. 14:13–21	Matt. 14:13–21	Matt. 14:13–21	Matt. 14:13–21

OLD TESTAMENT: ISAIAH 55:1–5

The theme of the great banquet or supper is one that occurs again and again in Scripture and is regularly enacted in the life of the church in the Lord's Supper. On each such occasion the church gathers to hear again the invitation and offer of life that is given as a present reality and to anticipate a time when all shall come to the Lord and be satisfied.

Isaiah 55:1–5 is one of the richest expressions of this theme in the Old Testament. It is essentially an invitation to life, one that was first addressed to a community of Judean exiles, a people who had experienced a kind of death of the spirit as the judgment of God had swept over them, destroying their homes and land and casting them into exile. The power of this text resides in the opening verses, which sound like the cries of an ancient water-seller or food-vendor hawking her wares in the marketplace. Two aspects of the style particularly convey that power. One is the heaping up of imperatives, calls to come, buy, eat. There are *twelve* imperatives in two and a half verses. The other feature of the mode of communication is the language of hunger and thirst, of buying and eating food to become revived. Such language is essentially metaphorical here, not unlike Jesus' words about "those who hunger and thirst after righteousness." By means of the repeated invitations and the food and drink imagery an intensity of effect is created, or perhaps more accurately, a sense of extravagance of offer that reminds one of contemporary advertisers on television or sweepstakes offers in the mail. The extravagance of the offer is enhanced by the indication that no money is necessary to buy in this market and by the extension of the offer to include not just the necessities but the really good and rich things (v. 2b). The climax of the repeated invitation is reached in vv. 2b–3a, where it moves from metaphorical imagery to the explicit divine invitation that is the point of the whole thing: "listen to me," "come to me." The accumulation of repeated calls and offers, together with the language that has to do with life and its sustenance and revival—all serve to bombard a thirsty-hungry "dead" people with the dinner call, and you don't even have to pay to get into the restaurant. All you do is come and listen.

The lesson thus makes an offer of life to those who even though they may not be dying are lifeless. There is no obligation upon those who respond to this insistent invitation. You cannot buy this gift, but you can waste a lot trying to find a life that satisfies. The source of this life for those who hunger and thirst is in listening and coming to the one who issues the invitation. Life itself is a gift, but here we are talking about a kind of life that is not automatically present within physical existence. Indeed the text assumes that many living do not have this life and long for it as the physically thirsty long for life-renewing water. Every person has experienced to some degree and at some time a terrible thirst and has known the sensation of good, of satisfaction, of rejuvenation and revival at its quenching. God's invitation to come is a call to come and receive that kind of satisfaction in the deepest recesses of our being.

What it means to respond to that invitation is indicated by this text in vv. 3b–5. The people hear that they are being called, invited, into covenant, an enduring relationship with God and a quality of life that is marked by God's grace and faithfulness—an abundance or richness that cannot be bought, only received (v. 3b). And through Israel and the manifestation of God's power and grace at work in this people the invitation goes out to others who will join with this community that comes to the Lord's Table and is richly sustained (vv. 4–5).

The lesson gives an ancient offer that is still good, an invitation to find in the free gift of a loving and gracious relationship to God the life that is worth living and for whose fullness and richness all hunger and thirst. That is a reality that is partly experienced and partly believed. Because it has to be believed in part to be experienced, many have turned down the invitation and gone away thirsty. Frederick Buechner expresses something of what this invitation is about in a more contemporary way:

> Grace is something you can never get but only be given. There's no way to earn it or deserve it or bring it about any more than you can deserve the taste of raspberries and cream or earn good looks or bring about your own birth. . . . A crucial eccentricity of the Christian faith is the assertion that people are saved by grace. There's nothing *you* have to do. There's nothing you *have* to do. There's nothing you have to *do*.[2]

The invitation is repeated again and again in Scripture. Jesus utters it in another form when he says, "Come to me, all who labor and are heavy laden, and I will give you rest" (Matt. 11:28). As the Bible closes, the invitation of Isa. 55:1 is repeated again and becomes an enduring part of the Christian vision of the kingdom of God: "I am the Alpha and the Omega, the beginning and the end. To the thirsty I will give from the fountain of the water of life without payment" (Rev. 21:6). The final chapter of Revelation then depicts "the river of the water of life, bright as crystal, flowing from the throne of God and of the Lamb" (Rev. 22:1), and near the very end issues one last time the invitation to partake of that water: "Let whoever is thirsty come, let whoever desires take the water of life without price" (Rev. 22:17; au. trans.).

GOSPEL: MATTHEW 14:13–21

The prophet of the exile issues the divine invitation to come and eat of the bread of life. In the Gospel lesson we are told of an occasion when Jesus indeed gave to the people around him bread to eat. It may be a surprising reversal for some to find the Old Testament lesson speaking of *metaphorical* bread of life and the Gospel lesson depicting Jesus offering *real* bread to people whose bodies craved food. Both lessons, however, are ultimately set to point us to the source of whatever nourishment our souls and bodies require.

The story of Jesus' feeding the five thousand is remembered in the Christian community as one of the great miracle stories of Jesus' ministry. It is not, however, told with a heavy weight on the miraculous aspect. No record is given of the crowd's astonishment at the feat of feeding so many with so little, a reaction that is customary in the miracle stories. Here the point is Jesus' sufficient feeding of hungry people. That is the bottom line, the thing that is to be remembered about this event: Many who were hungry found their need more than satisfied by Jesus' distribution of food.

As that point is clearly made, we learn some other things about this event. It arises out of the compassion of Jesus (v. 14), who sets always at the center of his ministry the physical circumstances and needs of other human beings. The fullness of life that Jesus offers in the Gospels is never apart from or ignorant of physical life, and no ministry carried out in his name nor any invitation for persons to find new life in commitment to him can diminish that compassion, or suggest that physical hunger and thirst and pain are not a part of the invitation of the one who says, "I am the bread of life; whoever comes to me shall not hunger, and whoever believes in me shall never thirst" (John 6:35; au. trans.).

In simple but direct fashion the story demonstrates that Jesus is able to provide for human needs in a way that others cannot. The disciples assume that the only way to feed the crowd is to send them into neighboring towns to look for food. Nor do they see their meager amount of food sufficient to provide when Jesus asks them to feed the crowd. Only Jesus is able to satisfy the needs of the people. Thus the story makes clear that here is one who offers a provision that others cannot give. Nor should the interpreter in this context miss the echo of Isa. 55:1 in Jesus' free provision of food and his refusal to send the people away to buy food.

Connected with this identification of the one who alone can provide is the dimension of the miraculous that, however muted, is still present in the story. There is something about the manner and abundance of Jesus' provision that transcends any human expectations and points beyond himself. "And taking the five loaves and the two fish he looked up to heaven, and blessed, and broke and gave the loaves to the disciples, and the disciples gave them to the crowds. And they all ate and were satisfied." Jesus' provision for human life is God's provision, and this meal in a lonely place is like every meal a reminder of where the gifts of and for life come from. It is also an anticipation in the Gospel story of that last meal that has become a continuing celebration in the Christian community of our communion together and with Christ and our partaking of the food and drink that are Christ's gifts to us and a source of renewal and revival as no other food and drink can ever be.

EPISTLE: ROMANS 8:35–39

No word of assurance, no testimony to the grace and love of God has ever sounded more clearly and unreservedly than these words of Paul. They are a bracket to the marvelous declaration of v. 28 and bring to a close the second section of his letter with "one of [Paul's] most eloquent passages of Christian comfort and assurance."[3] The conviction that the most dire experiences cannot negate or cancel out the love of God that is made known to us in Christ is set forth explicitly in these verses as we see from the catalogue of disasters listed by Paul in v. 35, most of which were experiences he himself had undergone at one time or another. Indeed by citing Ps. 44:22 he suggests that such assaults on human life—body and spirit—have been a regular feature of existence *coram Deo*—before God. Note that the text does not say, Who shall keep us from all harm? There are passages of Scripture that talk like that and they are to be listened to with great care. But Paul's word is almost a polar opposite. In this chapter and in these verses he says in effect, You can count on suffering of all sorts in your following Jesus, in your search for the kingdom of heaven. That has been my story and the story of many others. So expect trouble and suffering, poverty, prison, and persecution. Let the world throw all of that at us—and it will. They may harm us terribly. But there is nothing they can do that cuts us off from the love of Christ.

The final Christian assurance—final in the order of Paul's thought and in the experience of the Christian life—centers in the word that is repeated at the beginning and end of this lesson, "separate," and in the increasing intensity and inclusiveness of Paul's claim as he moves from the question, "Who shall separate us?" (v. 35) to the conclusion that "nothing will be able to sparate us" (v. 39). He asks first if all those kinds of terrible things that seem to make human existence disastrous, indeed less than human, full of pain and suffering, can keep us from being held forever by the loving hands of God. Then Paul drops the question form and moves to one of those powerful declarations that brook no questions in his own mind or from any outside source: "For I am sure. . . ." Here one senses that he is reaching out to identify any power in the universe, any time or space, any experience or perception that can possibly exist or be imagined. Whatever there may be, including death that seems to cut everything off, or even life, which is full of things that would seem capable of separating us from *God*, or any powers at work in the world, the unknown future, indeed *anything in the whole creation*—none of that is finally able, that is, has the power, to break the tie of love that binds us inextricably and irrevocably to God. Quite the contrary, as the middle verse (v. 37) of this lesson makes abundantly clear. That very love of Christ has given us a marvelous victory over all that would work to cut us off from the gift of love and grace that has been given to us in Christ Jesus our Lord. Everything about our life is contingent except that one thing—the love of God that holds us forever.

The lessons of this day speak of invitations to life in which all our hunger and thirst are satisfied and the gracious love of God is the controlling and indestructible ground of everything. The concluding words of Buechner's thoughts on grace cited above serve to bind these texts together and keep our thinking going:

> The grace of God means something like: Here is your life. You might never have been, but you *are* because the party wouldn't have been complete without you. Here is the world. Beautiful and terrible things will happen. Don't be afraid. I am with you. Nothing can ever separate us. It's for you I created the universe. I love you. There's only one catch. Like any other gift, the gift of grace can be yours only if you reach out and take it.
>
> Maybe being able to reach out and take it is a gift too.[4]

The Twelfth Sunday After Pentecost

Lutheran	Roman Catholic	Episcopal	Pres/UCC/Chr	Meth/COCU
1 Kings 19:9–18	1 Kings 19:9, 11–13a	Jon. 2:1–9	1 Kings 19:9–16	1 Kings 19:9–18
Rom. 9:1–5	Rom. 9:1–5	Rom. 9:1–5	Rom. 9:1–5	Rom. 9:1–5
Matt. 14:22–33	Matt. 14:22–33	Matt. 14:22–33	Matt. 14:22–33	Matt. 14:22–33

OLD TESTAMENT: 1 KINGS 19:9–18

The Old Testament lesson and the Gospel both tell us a story of a faithful disciple in a struggle of faith and doubt before the Lord. In the case of both Elijah and Peter, we look at persons who in the biblical story are exemplars of forthright commitment and faith (1 Kings 18 and Matt. 16:16)—Elijah the one faithful prophet left who stands on Mount Carmel against the four hundred prophets of Baal (1 Kings 18:22) and Peter the rock on which Jesus will build the church (Matt. 16:16–19). But both of these persons, as our lessons today remind us, are also among the clearest biblical examples of fearfulness and doubt (remember also Peter's denials of his Lord). In other words, as we read their full stories we are not simply given models of faith to marvel at or imitate but are told of the true struggle of faith in order that we may be instructed by it, or reassured by it, and that we may learn something of the shape of the Lord's response to those who have gone through such struggle in the past.

The words "faith" and "doubt" are appropriate for these stories. Jesus uses both of them in addressing Peter. The stories, however, make clear what the nature of faith and doubt is in the struggle and in so doing give us a clue to where that conflict is usually waged within the human spirit. The issue is between trust in the power and faithfulness of God and anxiety and fearfulness that God will not protect and care for the one who has made a commitment to the Lord. We are not dealing primarily with faith and doubt at the intellectual level of what can be believed about God but with the movement between a trusting confidence that is demonstrated in the midst of the vicissitudes of life and a fearful despair that crops up in just those same kinds of situations.

The story of Elijah on Mount Horeb (=Sinai) is a narrative counter to the story of his stand against the prophets of Baal on Mount Carmel. There, in defiance of the widespread apostasy of the people, the hostile and apostate King Ahab, the four hundred and fifty prophets of Baal, and the four hundred prophets of Asherah, Elijah declared, "I, even I only am left" (1 Kings 18:22) and challenged the prophets to evoke the power of *their god* as he knew *the Lord* would respond to his prayers. In chapter 19 Elijah utters the same words, "I even I only am left," twice (vv. 10, 14) at Horeb, only now they are no longer the words of a brave prophet trusting in the power of the Lord against great odds but an expression of lonely fear before the threat of a single but powerful individual, Queen Jezebel. The prophetic public declaration of obedience has now turned into an inner doubt, depression, and despair. The one who stood tall has now become afraid and self-pitying.

The familiar part of this passage is vv. 12–13, the report of the apparent theophany of wind, earthquake, and fire followed by "the sound of silence" and the voice of the Lord that speaks to Elijah as he comes out to the cave's entrance. One must be careful not to overplay this part of the story or seek its essential meaning in these verses. They are part of a larger whole whose center is the repeated dialogue between the Lord and Elijah. The theophanic elements are in this case a counter to what they have meant in the past. If Elijah is in some fashion identified with Moses (see Exodus 32—34), he is not a repeat performance. The natural paraphernalia of revelation, whether of Baal or the Lord, do not in this case serve that purpose. Nor does the Lord deal with this inner and personal struggle of faith as with the previous public conflict of faith in chapter 18. The Lord sent the fire then, but not this time. For the one who has been chosen and commissioned, who has been the obedient agent of the Lord's power in the past, the fireworks of theophany are not the vehicle of the Lord's dealing. One is reminded of Jeremiah's complaints and the Lord's response to get back in the fray. In the face of Elijah's fear and depression neither a revelatory sound and light show nor a therapeutic counseling program are what is given.

Instead the fear and doubt of the prophet evoke a simple and direct challenge and a renewal of his commission, a re-call to his task as a prophet. This is as direct a word to the obedient and now doubting prophet as was his word and the fire to the people at Mount Carmel. The Lord's question, "What are you doing here, Elijah?" is an example of what we find not infrequently in Scripture, a divine questioning that is an implicit critique of choices that have been made, directions taken. The aroused fears of Elijah are real. He is in danger, and he is not given spectacular reassurance. But neither is the Lord's agent allowed easily to wallow in self-pity or give up his vocation. The divine call continues; the prophetic burden is to be borne. In a fashion that cuts against the grain of our modern ethos, depression, despair, and self-pity are not acceptable for the servants of the Lord.

There is, of course, a kind of therapy here for this burnt-out prophet, as one interpreter has described him, though not perhaps therapy in the way we usually use the term. It is in the divine instruction to get back to work. We know nothing of the restoration of Elijah's spirits, only of his resumption of the prophetic task: "Go . . . , and he went" (vv. 15, 19). It is a familiar model of the divine word and human response (cf. Gen. 12:1, 4a; Amos 7:15) and it is an essential lesson of the text. Further, there is a kind of assurance given also. For despite his sense of lonely obedience, Elijah is not in fact alone. There are seven thousand in Israel who also remain obedient to the Lord, and it is with this faithful Israel that the prophet may now join hands in the difficult and unpleasant times that lie ahead.

GOSPEL: MATTHEW 14:22–33

As with the "still small voice" of 1 Kings 19, it is possible for the miraculous elements of this story to move to the center and occupy our attention unduly. The interpreter would do best neither to try to explain the miracle of Jesus walking on the water nor to defend it but to focus on the story and what it seems to say to the church. For it is indeed a story for and about the church, represented here by the disciples. And it is, as we have said, a story about the inner conflict between faith and doubt, between a trusting confidence in the power of the Lord and a fearfulness that the forces and powers around us are too strong and will undo us.

As in the account of Elijah on Mount Carmel and Mount Horeb, we see two sides of these disciples and are led to believe that is the way with disciples. In a single episode their obedient trust (vv. 28, 33) is laid alongside anxious fear and doubt (vv. 26, 30–31). Within the span of these few verses they move from terror to trust and back again to fear and then once more to obedient worship. Such a continuum—and it continues as the story goes on—is surely indicative of the shape of the church's response to its Lord.

The text is filled with indications that the Lord of the church is its sure anchor in whatever storms arise. That is one of the plain—not allegorical—meanings of the text. In the dark of the night, when the strong winds blow—literally or figuratively—the risen Lord is there with the words, "Take heart, it is I; have no fear," words capable of stilling both the anxious heart and the raging wind, as our story makes clear. That is a word to be taken most seriously. The text implies that the disciples trusted it, and we are to hear that implication for the way of discipleship.

This trust in the Lord's power against the inner and outer storms is explicitly articulated in the words of that representative disciple, Peter: "Lord, if it is you, bid me come to you on the water." Peter believes the word of the Lord can be trusted, and he will risk everything in obedience to that word. What marvelous faith! Indeed it is, and let us not lose sight of that point as we realize it is not the last word about Peter here. For Peter's confident venture into the waters turns to fear when the winds blow. Eduard Schweizer has pointedly described the intention of the story at this point:

> When faith devotes its attention strictly to the word of Jesus, it may take a realistic view of wind and waves, but must not allow them to distract it. According to Matthew, such faith is promised everything; but when it begins to vacillate between the command of its Lord and some evident personal danger, it falters.[5]

At this point the resonance of the Gospel with the Elijah story is most clear. The obedient prophet and disciple lose heart in the face of the realization of danger. Like Elijah, Peter's doubt and fear evoke a divine response. Neither individual is abandoned when faith is at its nadir. Peter receives two replies to his despairing cry. The fundamental one is a saving hand and the assurance that the Lord will not let a disciple sink beneath the waters even when faith has weakened. But there is also, like the Lord's question to Elijah, a rebuke that is addressed to any disciple who weakens before the difficulties that arise in the way of obedience.

The stories of Elijah and the disciples are not an easy lesson. As they set a mirror before our living between faith and doubt, confidence and despair, they forthrightly challenge the tendency to fall into fear and doubt and call them into question for those who bear the prophetic burden or walk the way of discipleship. But they also make clear we are not left alone in such situations, for we hear of both the Lord's delivering help in the face of despair and the renewed instruction to take up the task that the Lord has set. Let that be the comforting and tough lesson of our preaching these texts.

EPISTLE: ROMANS 9:1–5

These verses begin a three-chapter discussion by Paul of God's election of Israel and the relation of that divine choice to the election of all, Jew and Gentile, in Christ. It is a most crucial part of Paul's overall theology and fundamental to Christian thinking about Jews, about Israel past and present, and their place in the redemptive work of God. The continuing argument of these chapters is complex, but the basic notes that are sounded here are clear and reiterated in some fashion again and again in the verses that follow.

First, *Paul really cares about his fellow Jews' positive response to the Messiah who has come.* One who has known the transforming joy of the gospel as the outcome of God's redemptive work in human history cannot help but be anguished when the elect of God do not also respond and see what is so clear and true to him, that all the promises of God have their yea and amen in Christ. Paul's anguish and willingness to be cut off himself from the elect if that were to bring about the affirmative response of the Jews are the measurement of how much that matters. He is not indifferent to anyone's failure to hear clearly the good news at the heart of the universe, especially those who have always been its recipients.

Second, the special benefits God has given to the Jews are real and enduring. Nothing that has happened has changed that. They are "my brethren," "Israelites" (this is a theological election term). To them *still belong* all those things Paul mentions in vv. 4–5, especially the promises and the fact that the Christ has come from their midst. None of this is taken away.

Third, the word of God and the promises of God do not fail. That is the primary point that Paul wishes to make, as his discussion in the following verses makes clear. The reaction of God's people can never undo that. The whole Old Testament confirms that, and we see it, for example, in the Old Testament lesson today where in the face of national apostasy the Lord continues on with the faithful remnant of seven thousand and the prophet is sent back to the task. Matters really are ultimately in God's hands. The promises, the choices, the purposes are God's. The continuity of the Lord's chosen people is by the gracious election of God that interacts with all sorts of human responses but is not broken by them or dependent upon biological and racial connections. All are connected to that history only by God's gracious promise, which is never taken back nor defeated by rejection.

As the Gospel and the Old Testament lessons place us in the center of the struggle between trust and fearfulness, so now the Epistle places us in the middle of Paul's anguish about the response to God by those whom God has chosen and his great confidence in the power of God to carry out the divine purpose through the elect of God.

The Thirteenth Sunday After Pentecost

Lutheran	Roman Catholic	Episcopal	Pres/UCC/Chr	Meth/COCU
Isa. 56:1, 6–8	Isa. 56:1, 6–7	Isa. 56:1 (2–5), 6–7	Isa. 56:1–7	Isa. 56:1–8
Rom. 11:13–15, 29–32	Rom. 11:13–15, 29–32	Rom. 11:13–15, 29–32	Rom. 11:13–16, 29–32	Rom. 11:13–16, 29–32
Matt. 15:21–28	Matt. 15:21–28	Matt. 15:21–28	Matt. 15:21–28	Matt. 15:21–28

EPISTLE: ROMANS 11:13–15, 29–32

The lessons of this Sunday have their common ground in the issue that occupies Paul's attention in Romans 9—11: the relation of Israel and the Gentiles in the gracious purposes of God. In these verses from chapter 11 Paul's explanation of that relationship reaches its conclusion and scores some of its basic points. While the argument as a whole involves a relatively complex presentation of the history of salvation and the place of Israel and the Gentiles in past, present, and future stages of that history, the essential theological conclusion is found in

v. 32. The repeated "all" underscores the fact that Jew and Gentile alike have been given the freedom to resist and disobey the gracious purpose of God and thus incur God's judgment that there is no way out of resistance and disobedience except by God's mercy. But then that is the point of everything, even human rejection—to uncover the inexpressible mercy of God!

Within the extended discussion that reaches this conclusion some important directions are given to Christians about how they live with and think about Israel and the Jews, who share with them both a rejection of God and the mercy of God. One of these directions is the realization that neither in theological perspective nor in human relationships is there any place whatsoever for anti-Semitism or anti-Judaism. Paul talks about Israel as hardened and rejecting, indeed as "enemies" of God (v. 28), a category derived from the psalms of Israel and the cries of Israelites for help against those who would do them in. But all of that is within the plan of God and only temporary. What is lasting and permanent is Israel's status as God's "beloved" (v. 28) and Paul's "my brethren" (9:3). Anti-Semitism has no basis *anthropologically* because we are all children of God, created in God's image—a fact that the church has learned from Israel. It has no basis *morally* because of the law of love and the inclusive understanding of who are our neighbors, our brothers and sisters, that we learn from Jesus in the parable of the Good Samaritan. Finally, anti-Semitism has no basis *theologically* because even an Israel that rejects and is subject to the wrath of God is forever beloved of God, recipients of the irrevocable gifts and call of God.

Instead of inappropriate and unacceptable anti-Judaism the Epistle lesson leads Christians toward a kind of strange and humble gratitude that our knowledge of the glory of God in Christ is directly an outcome of Israel's relationship to God, both its rejection and its acceptance. Karl Barth, who has given extended attention to these chapters and the issue of election in his *Church Dogmatics*, has emphasized this point:

> However it may be with that hardening of the rest of Israel, however it may be with Israel's transgression . . . , Israel is still the possession and work of God, and as such the presupposition without which there would be no Church, and no Gentile Christians. No matter what may have to be said about those who are hardened, they, too, are part of this possession and work of God to which the Church and its Gentile Christian members also owe everything.[6]

Finally, in all of this story of Israel and the Gentiles, of church and synagogue, the operative factor is the triumphant grace and mercy of God. In the purpose of God the salvation of the Gentiles, which happened out of the fact that the majority of the Jews rejected Jesus as the Messiah, shall be met and become an even greater reality by the restoration of Israel. What Paul is finally speaking about is a kind of irresistible grace, a merciful purpose that works in and through both rejection and acceptance. Any preaching of this text will need to focus primary attention on *the centrality of the mercy of God* (repeated four times in vv. 30–32) in all that happens with the church and with Israel and the sense that the responses of both are incorporated within *the good purposes of God.*

GOSPEL: MATTHEW 15:21–28

The story of the encounter between Jesus and the Canaanite woman is a hard one to read and appropriate because it does not paint a very attractive portrait of Jesus. Notions of him as kind and open to all, impressions that are constantly undergirded in the Gospels generally, are not apparently confirmed in this story where he harshly puts down a woman's approach because she is not a Jew. Listening to the story in the context of Paul's discussion of the election of Jew and Gentile and God's merciful purpose in Jesus Christ may be the only—or at least the best—context for dealing with the difficulties we encounter in this text.

Since the most obvious difficulty is the portrayal of Jesus, an interpretation of the text needs to give some accounting of that. Two avenues present themselves. One is historical, that is, a recognition that in this story, and especially in its Matthean version, we encounter a retrojection backward of the later controversies in the church about whether or not the Gentiles were to be the object of mission on the part of the disciples of Jesus. His harsh words are a strong reflection of the priority of the Jewish context for his ministry and that of those who came after him.

It is more helpful and plausible to view Jesus' words in the context of the narrative movement of the pericope. The initial verses make crystal clear that we are off the beaten track, outside Jesus' normal paths of ministry. Jesus is neither in Judea nor Samaria. He is in Phoenicia (Tyre and Sidon). Furthermore the narrator does not say simply that a woman came to him, but that a *Canaanite* woman came for help. In the Old Testament, of course, this is the term par excellence for those with whom Israelites were to have no contact. The story, therefore, quite self-consciously sets up the woman as a total outsider with whom Jesus would naturally have no association and vice versa. The sequence of the woman's cries for help—three times she calls him "Lord"—and Jesus' two strong responses serve to build and heighten the point and climax of the story: the tenacious faith of this one who would be expected to have no interest in and nothing to do with the Jew Jesus and his strong response of acceptance and healing. Jesus' final words would not be so enthusiastic apart from the previous resistance and her refusal to accept it. His harsh questions have brought out the unswerving trust she has in him in a way that a simple miracle story could not. That trust, which pushes open the door to Jesus' healing power, is as much or more the point of the story than the healing itself. One cannot help but hear this story against the previous Gospel lesson. There the confidence of an intimate disciple of Jesus gives way in the face of trouble. Here a cry for help arises out of a dogged trust that persists even when Jesus himself appears to cut the ground out from under it. From just such an example the church learns something about what real faith in Jesus is—which is exactly the point of Jesus' final words.

So the Gospel shows us something of the tenacity of faith where we least expect it and creates a double surprise by the Lord's initial rejections and then his sudden extravagant acceptance. But the story still bears also its relation to the point that Paul makes in Romans 9—11: the coming of Jesus was to Israel first and then to the Gentiles. It illustrates Paul's double point that Jesus is from the Jews and for the Jews and that those who are Gentiles have been drawn into the circle of faith only by relationship to God's story with Israel. That will always be the case. This Gospel story, however, makes clear what has never been so evident before, that *Canaanites* (read also Gentiles) can be and have been incorporated into the story of Israel and by faith are recipients of the healing grace of God. In the Old Testament such a reality is *anticipated* as a manifestation of the kingdom of God, as we see from the Old Testament lesson.

Do not leave your communication of the Gospel without some direct focus on the Canaanite woman. She is an assertive woman, a model of faith, who in a tenacious concern for her daughter's health refuses to be put off from the one source that she is confident can give help. We would call her response impudence; Jesus calls it great faith.

OLD TESTAMENT: ISAIAH 56:1, 6–8

The doors of the church are open! That is one of the primary notes that is sounded in the lessons for this Pentecost Sunday, and it is an echo of the reality of Pentecost itself. The Old Testament foundation for our understanding that the doors of the church cannot be closed to some people and some groups is laid in this great text from Isaiah. Alongside the Canaanite woman of the Gospel text stand the eunuch and the foreigner, and as we see them, we know that in some sense the walls of partition, at least from God's side, are truly broken down. We cannot fully feel the force of that without recognizing that people in all three of these categories are specifically those who had been *formerly excluded*—by the Lord's command. The Book of Deuteronomy indicates in a number of places, for example, its abhorrence of everything Canaanite in the worship of the Lord, as well as the specific exclusion of the foreigner from the benefits of the law (e.g., Deut. 15:1–6; 17:15) and the eunuch from the assembly of the Lord (Deut. 23:1–2).

Now a totally new way is set forth. The community that worships the Lord becomes fully open to all ("for my house shall be called a house of prayer *for all peoples*"). The radical character of that new situation, however, is underscored by the fact that this openness does not stay on the general level but is exemplified in the accessibility of the previously excluded eunuch and foreigner. We encounter here a break with the notion that God's elect are delimited by kinship, birth, and race. Whereas the community of Israel had been expected to be righteous and obedient to the Lord, righteousness and obedience now define who belongs to the community of Israel. The implications of that for the way the community of faith defines itself are large. The seeds of the Gentile mission on the part of those Jews who followed Jesus are clearly sown by this text.

In the proclamation of these matters three things should be kept in view and have their impact on our preaching.

First, in Israel's own history a tension existed between the call for the openness of the assembly of the Lord to all peoples and an insistence on continued delimitation on grounds other than devotion to the Lord.

The chuch has continued to fight that battle in its own life throughout the course of its history. Inclusiveness may be assumed, but within the last twenty years in this country the doors of the church have been shut and people kept out on the basis of race rather than commitment. One cannot assume that this word is clear and the issue settled once for all. In preaching and congregational life the doors must be kept open.

Second, the specificity of this text in identifying those who may belong to the worshiping community should not be lost in its proclamation. While the generalization "all peoples" is given, the detailed elaboration is about the foreigner and the eunuch. Just such concrete identification of those who in some fashion have been kept outside the gates of the house of the Lord needs to be made so that the text may not be perceived as simply a pleasant word but can have its continuing power to open doors that the church quietly keeps locked.

Third, the proper tension in the text is between the invitation to come to the feast and the call to discipleship, between the breakdown of any a priori definition of who may belong to the assembly of the Lord and the insistence that whoever belongs to the community that worships the Lord is under obligation to hold fast to God's covenant (v. 6), to keep justice and do righteousness (v. 1).

The Fourteenth Sunday After Pentecost

Lutheran	Roman Catholic	Episcopal	Pres/UCC/Chr	Meth/COCU
Exod. 6:2–8	Isa. 22:15, 19–23	Isa. 51:1–6	Isa. 22:19–23	Isa. 22:19–23
Rom. 11:33–36	Rom. 11:33–36	Rom. 11:33–36	Rom. 11:33–36	Rom. 11:33–36
Matt. 16:13–20	Matt. 16:13–20	Matt. 16:13–20	Matt. 16:13–20	Matt. 16:13–20

The Old Testament and Epistle lessons on this Sunday focus our attention very much on God. They are highly theological, one (Romans) a paean of praise to the unfathomable greatness and mystery that is God, the other (Exodus) God's opening up of that mystery in self-revelation to the people who are to carry out God's way in the world. The Gospel shifts attention to a human figure, Peter, but here also we see that the text has to do with God's revelation to those who are to be God's people in the world. The authority that is given to Peter is both an outgrowth of the revelation and an indication, in part, of how the mysterious ways of God shall be carried out in the very human institution of the church.

EPISTLE: ROMANS 11:33–36

There is of course no set way in which the lectionary texts must be viewed logically in relation to each other. Indeed on any given Sunday one may come at them or construct their logical interrelationships in different but legitimate ways. It is at least appropriate in this case where the texts speak so much about God to suggest that our starting point is an unavoidable and openly declared agnosticism before the transcendent mystery that is God.

Christian preaching and teaching and the ministry and mission of the church often are only one step away from an arrogant triumphalism and not infrequently fall over into a claim to know securely the ways of God in the world. The only safeguards against such tendencies are humble awareness of the mystery of God and the impulse to give praise to God rather than speak for God. Paul, who has spoken much for God, ends now in praise and affirmation of God's unsearchability. Paul teaches about God, but equally important, he models a proper theological humility, aware that when even the deepest theological doctrines have been worked out and the ways of God thoroughly explained and justified, there still is no one who "knows the mind of the Lord" or "has been his counselor" (Isa. 40:13, quoted in Rom. 11:34). No one needs to be reminded of this fact more than those of us entrusted with the tasks of instruction and preaching, who find ourselves having to deal with theological mysteries and need always to remember that they really *are* theological mysteries, that the very subject matter of theology is unsearchable and inscrutable, the source and means and goal of everything (v. 36). Thus the Epistle has to do with the subject matter of our preaching—the transcendent majesty and mystery of God—and with its style—humility before God and glorification of God.

Two things, at least, are of some importance in hearing this text. One is the realization that Paul's hymnic testimony to the inscrutability of God's ways is not simply out of the blue, unconnected to anything else.

It is the final outcome of his long discussion of God's way with Israel and its relation to the church. Earlier Paul has called this a "mystery" (11:25) and has endeavored to help explain it. Now in conclusion he says that with all his explanation—which he clearly holds to—there is much that is beyond all our understanding. So, on this question, that is, on the place of Israel and the church, Jew and Gentile, in the redemptive and providential work of God, there is much that we can never comprehend. Let us not therefore claim too much to know "the mind of the Lord," the judgments and ways of God with regard to Israel or even our own place in the divine economy.

The further inference from the text is both theological and pastoral. God's inscrutability is often perceived or felt as the grounds for passivity or acceptance of the threatening contingency of human existence. Here, however, Paul's recognition of the fact that God's ways and judgments are beyond examination or even comprehension has a quite opposite intention and effect. What Paul is celebrating and giving praise for is a divine work whose mystery and incomprehensibility lie in God's unbelievable grace and wisdom. The term "riches" in this context (9:23; 10:12) and generally in Paul (Rom. 2:4; Phil. 4:19) refers to God's kindness and mercy. That is what is so deep, beyond fathoming. If one knows that God is in charge and bent or directed toward a way of merciful kindness—both convictions clearly confirmed to Paul in the gospel of Jesus Christ—then the knowledge and wisdom of God are a source of great joy precisely because they are beyond our figuring out and encompass us in immeasurable and unfailing mercy.

The heart of the matter in this text—and especially as a conclusion to Paul's complex thoughts on Israel and the Gentiles—is well expressed by C. E. B. Cranfield in these words:

> Paul has certainly not provided neat answers to the baffling questions which arise in connexion with the subject matter of these three chapters [Romans 9—11]. He has certainly not swept away all the difficulties. But, if we have followed him through these chapters with serious and open-minded attentiveness, we may well feel that he has given us enough to enable us to repeat the "Amen" of his doxology in joyful confidence that the deep mystery which surrounds us is neither a nightmare mystery of meaninglessness nor a dark mystery of arbitrary omnipotence but the mystery which will never turn out to be anything other than the mystery of the altogether good and merciful and faithful God.[7]

The psalmist anticipates Paul's sense of the richness and inscrutability of God's ways—and provides our bridge into the Old Testament—with these words:

> How precious to me are thy thoughts, O God!
> How vast is the sum of them!
>
> (Ps. 139:17)

OLD TESTAMENT: EXODUS 6:2–8

Paul dares to sing a song of joy over the mystery of God's ways because he knows that however inscrutable they are, they have always been gracious. There is a consistent character to them that can be counted upon. How does he know that? Equally important, how do *we* know that?

Romans 9—11, of course, gives some considerable answer to that and points, as always, to the gracious and redeeming work of God in Jesus Christ. The consistency or the faithfulness of the Lord in all God's mysterious ways, however, is seen only in the whole biblical story reaching all the way back to the beginnings. That is what the Old Testament lesson clearly shows. The mystery that is the transcendent God is beyond our searchings and always will be, but God's self-revelation has let us see something of the way that mystery is involved with us.

The disclosed yet hidden God is a feature of the very opening words of this text in which the Lord speaks of an appearance to the patriarchs under a different name. The revelation of the new name "the Lord" is a disclosure, a clue to the nature of the reality that undergirds the universe. But it is a *clue*, not a full uncovering of the mystery, as we discern both from the fact that God has appeared to others under other names and from the mystery that clearly shrouds the name "Yahweh" (=the Lord) when it is given in Exod. 3:13–15. The continuing puzzlement and debate about this name is not a testimony to lack of data or scholarly ingenuity. Both are present in good measure. The story itself insists on an inscrutability ("I am who I am" or "I will be what I will be") in the name as a reflection of God's inscrutability. It also suggests that as you watch the story that unfolds and listen to the divine words that initiate it, you will learn something of the shape of this mystery that is the source and ground of everything (Rom. 11:36).

So in this text at the beginning of the great redemptive event of Israel's history, we are given some indication of God's profile and why it is Paul can rejoice before the mystery and be confident of its character. Notes are sounded here that shall echo throughout the story till its as yet unknown end. The first of those notes is the clear indication that God is responsive to human suffering ("I have *heard* the *groaning* of the people of Israel . . . I will *bring you out* from under *the burdens of the Egyptians* . . . I will *deliver you* from *their bondage*"). In this case it is specifically the ones with whom the Lord has entered into covenant whose suffering is removed, but the biblical story not only identifies God's delivering work in behalf of other peoples (Amos 9:7) but places at its center the claim that in the death and resurrection of Jesus Christ, God has identified with and, in the mystery of God's powerful grace, acted in behalf of all who suffer. If there is an illumination given to us into the darkness of God's ways, it is here. The extent to which Psalm 22 and Isaiah 53 provide the hermeneutical key to the New Testament understanding of the passion of Jesus is a confirmation of this word of God's involvement in human suffering.

Indeed the Exodus texts (chaps. 3 and 6) suggest that the Lord is one who comes out of the mystery and is made known in the context of oppression and the cry of the victims (v. 7b). Elie Wiesel in his memoir of the Nazi death camps, *Night*, tells one of the most terrible stories of all the nightmares to come out of those experiences. Forced to watch a thirteen-year-old boy suffer a slow, agonizing death by hanging, Wiesel came to the conclusion that he was, in some fashion, watching the death of God on that gallows, and faith in God was no longer possible for him. Christians have very little claim to make in the face of the Holocaust of the Jews. But if there is anything to hold onto, it is the conviction that in some inscrutable and unfathomable way, God *was* dying with that boy. The exodus story and the resurrection bid us trust that such suffering-with is God's intention, but not God's final word. "I am the Lord and I will deliver you."

So the notes sound on and on of the Lord's purpose to loose the chains and bonds that enslave people (cf. Luke 4:16–21). There is much that is unsearchable in God's way of doing that with Israel and with others, but Paul's word still holds good that the depth into which we look is not finally a black abyss but "the depth of the riches and wisdom and knowledge of God."

The other notes we hear prominently in the text are two. One is of God's purpose to establish a people out of these redeemed suffering ones. They shall be those who live in relation to and in worship of the Lord of all (Rom. 11:36); they shall also be those who are set to demonstrate and keep the Lord's way of justice and righteousness in the world (Gen. 18:19). In this sense the text speaks to us about what it means to be the Israel of God. The final note to pick up is the one that both Paul and the Old Testament affirm again and again: the faithfulness of God. Here it is present in the word of God's *establishing* and *remembering* the covenant with Israel. That is a way of saying God never lets go and will always be faithful. And it is why one can sing hymns of joy while bowing before the mystery.

GOSPEL: MATTHEW 16:13–20

The revelation of God's way continues as a theme for this Sunday with Peter's great confession. The text underscores the fact that such disclosure of the heart of God's purpose, the recognition of the Lord's anointed, is not a matter of human deduction ("flesh and blood") but can only come through the revelation of the transcendent one ("my Father who is in heaven," v. 17). The biblical witness is fairly clear and consistent on this point. While faith always seeks understanding and so can and should pursue the theological enterprise vigorously and with all the tools at its disposal, faith always comes as a gift. Yet that gift, when received, is the stuff out of which a church is built. Jesus' words preserve a strong tension between the divine work and the human work. Peter is the human focus of this story, and his position is such that an institution as powerful and important in the church as the papacy has been built largely on the basis of Jesus' words. But both Peter's confession and the church that is built on this rock are specifically said to be the work of God (v. 17) and the Christ ("*I* will build *my* church . . . *I* will give you the keys of the kingdom of heaven . . .). This tension between the revelation and work of God and the earthen vessel, the human vehicle through which both are carried out, is a familiar biblical theme and an appropriate emphasis for the proclamation of this text. The incarnational mystery, which is present not only in *the* incarnation but in all its further manifestations, for example, the church as the body of Christ, is heightened by virtue of the fact that the "rock" in this instance can and does become a stone of stumbling (cf. Peter as the *skandalon* in Matt. 16:23 and his later denials). Peter is a paradigm of both the possibilities and the problems of God's unsearchable ways coming to light and life in the church (cf. Acts 1 as a further example). It is through just such ones as this that Christ's work in the church is carried out. That is one of the most inscrutable of all God's ways. Yet it is not ultimately a source of anxiety, for "the powers of death [or: the gates of hell] shall not prevail against it."

The word of Christ's authority conveyed to Peter (and by implication leaders of the church who follow in his train) is a serious one to be received with fear and trembling as a word to contemporary leaders. It means that there is an authentic representation of Christ in our leadership, and not simply an authority by the church and its members. One can only represent such authority in humility and the continuing search for the mind of Christ. Further, an abuse of such authority is in some sense a betrayal of the one who has laid this foundation and given the authority. Some denominations have as their Old Testament lesson for this Sunday the text in Isa. 22:19–23. It is a helpful reminder to us that representative authority can be taken away—a caution against any assumptions about any of us ever possessing a perpetual and absolute authority in behalf of Christ.

The Fifteenth Sunday After Pentecost

Lutheran	Roman Catholic	Episcopal	Pres/UCC/Chr	Meth/COCU
Jer. 15:15–21	Jer. 20:7–9	Jer. 15:15–21	Jer. 20:7–9	Jer. 15:15–21
Rom. 12:1–8	Rom. 12:1–2	Rom. 12:1–8	Rom. 12:1–7	Rom. 12:1–8
Matt. 16:21–26	Matt. 16:21–27	Matt. 16:21–27	Matt. 16:21–28	Matt. 16:21–28

The lessons for this Sunday offer much scriptural material for rich and faithful preaching, notably in their focus on the death of Jesus and its place in the gracious purpose of God (Matt. 16:21–23, 27–28) and in Paul's words about spiritual gifts (Rom. 12:1–8). What holds these texts together, however, and can be the focus for preaching on them as a whole or individually is perhaps best exemplified in the "therefore" of Rom. 12:1. Here, in other words, are the implications of hearing and responding to the call of God, of receiving the gifts of God's redeeming grace. The primary focus of the Scripture lessons this Sunday is on *the Christian life* with particular emphasis on the nature of the demand, the cost of discipleship for those who commit themselves to the way of the Lord.

EPISTLE: ROMANS 12:1–8

Paul's word, "therefore," presents itself as a starting point. First of all, one hears the indissoluble tie between faith and practice, between God's redemptive mercy and God's expectations for the life of those who have come to know and experience that mercy. The proclamation of the text will seek to convey something of this two-part structure of Christian existence, one that Paul unfolds regularly in his letters. One of the most interesting and significant features of his presentation here is the way in which both God's act in Jesus Christ and our response in Christian life are caught up in the single word "grace." That grace of God is what Paul has been explicating with passion and profundity for eleven chapters. Now, however, he speaks of the possibilities of our response and our participation in the household of faith also as grace, twice referring to "the grace given to me/us" (vv. 3, 6). The force of such a move on Paul's part is to translate the structure of Christian existence into grace and to identify both God's call and our faithful response as *gifts* of God.

The redemptive love of God, the measure or degree of faith that each Christian has (v. 3b), and the gifts for service in the church—all of this is *given* to us by God. No pride in our human accomplishments is justified, only thanksgiving and the proper use of whatever gifts (degree or kind) have been given to us. What a marvelously freeing word that is! We are not called to live up to some human standard or self-image, but only to use the gifts. But that indeed we are to do, by the grace that is given to us. Humble faithfulness may or may not be prized among the possible human virtues generally recognized in the human community. In the community of faith that is shaped in every way by God's grace, it may be what matters most.

What Paul sees as an outcome of the experience of God's grace in Jesus Christ is a kind of total *transformation of our lives.* Here Paul uses some rather concrete and vivid language that is not typically part of his vocabulary. He instructs Christians to stop being conformed to this world, that is, to cease being poured into the mold of this world so that we come out shaped into the patterns, the configurations of the world around us. Rather we are to undergo a *metamorphosis* (so the Greek for "transformation"), defined in one dictionary as "a striking alteration in appearance, character, or circumstances." In its frequent biological usage, metamorphosis refers to a marked and more or less abrupt change in form or structure, as well as habits, of an animal, as, for example, the change of a tadpole into a frog. The Christian life is an ongoing but marked transformation of that sort, as if one put on a whole new set of clothes (for some of us that would include eyeglasses and a new hairstyle). It is a transformation from one way of thinking to a new way of thinking ("the renewal of your mind"). We are accustomed to speaking about a Christian style of life, patterns of behavior, and action. Paul clearly has that in mind, as the rest of the chapter indicates. But in these verses we must not miss his concern not only for our actions but for the way we think, what is in our minds. That is the primary focus in vv. 2–3. Our minds are made new and so we think and act differently. Paul describes that new way of thinking as one that thinks in terms of God's will, here explained generally as what is good, acceptable, and perfect.

We gain some further clues about this metamorphosis of the mind in Paul's letter to the Christians at Philippi (Phil. 2:1–11). There he speaks for a common mind in the community, a way of thinking that comes from Christ Jesus, who, though in the "form" of God, emptied himself taking the "form" of a servant, and being found in human "form," humbled himself and became obedient unto death. As the other lessons of this Sunday serve to underscore, it is this way of thinking—a Christ-shaped humility and obedience to God's will at whatever price—that is the new mind, the new mold, the new set of clothes put on by Christians.

Both the passage in Romans and the passage in Philippians place at the center of this new way of thinking a transformed mind. This new mind breaks out of the world's mold enabling a different way of thinking about *self.* Humility nurtured in community is the aim of this transformation (vv. 3–8). When all the gifts are from God, ego can be transformed into an appropriate awareness of self that discerns one's proper place in the community, one's true gifts to be given over to the service of others and the good of the whole. This is why Christian faith is not ultimately an individualistic religion. Its primary images of church, body, and kingdom reflect the fact that individual existence in this world and any other worlds there may be is ultimately meant to be a part of a larger whole, a community of selves who become one in the service of God. That is the essential point of T. S. Eliot's choruses from "The Rock" summarized in the lines:

> What life have you if you have not life together?
> There is no life that is not in community
> and no community not lived in praise of GOD.[8]

GOSPEL: MATTHEW 16:21–28

A way of thinking about self is also at the center of Jesus' words about discipleship. That it is not an ordinary word or an easy word is immediately indicated by Peter's reaction to Jesus' teaching about his passion. The one to whom the very nature of Jesus' relationship to God has been revealed so that he has confessed it openly cannot take the word about a suffering way. When Jesus says to Peter, "You are not on the side of God" he uses the same verb that Paul uses several times in Rom. 12:3 to speak about how the Christian ought to *think* and in Phil. 2:5 about having the "*mind*, among yourselves, which is yours in Christ Jesus. . . ." Jesus' rebuke to Peter is, therefore, precisely a rebuke of his way of thinking and a call for a change of mind, from being oriented toward the world's way to a setting of the mind and heart on the things of God. In some ways both Jesus and Paul are calling for a kind of *metanoia*, a turning or converting of the mind to a different mind-set, that is, a mind set on the will and way of God, which with regard to the self, the ego, is radically different from the normal human mind-set. Jesus rebukes Peter sharply because he knows Peter's words are a genuine temptation for him to think like, to set his heart on, to conform to, this world and its tendency to place self at the center.

The figure of Peter is an obvious entree into the proclamation of this text and need not be resisted. He is representative of the disciples, but not just of the original band. The mix of devotion to Christ, willingness to work in his behalf, and forthright confession of faith, together with fearfulness, betrayal, and resistance to the demands of Jesus' way is certainly not peculiar to this disciple. He is a mirror in which many of us have seen and will see our own self-image if we are honest enough. The issue of mind-set, which Jesus put to Peter, is there before everyone who would be a follower of Jesus, and all of us are drawn to set ourselves on human things rather than the things of God, to resist the possibility that obedience to God's way may be painful and destructive of self.

So Jesus calls Peter back to a position of discipleship ("Get behind me") and begins to teach him and all other disciples—then and now—what that discipleship properly and of necessity involves, what it means to respond to the call of Christ. Among those implications of what Bonhoeffer has properly called "the cost of discipleship," I would single out the following. First, responding to the call of Christ is not easy; there is a cost. Denial of self is not the same thing as self-enhancement. Indeed, it is its opposite. To pursue the way of love, to work for God's kingdom of peace and justice, to place the welfare and good of others ahead of our own—none of that is easy, and we do a disservice to ourselves and to others when we portray the call of Christ as one that is relatively easy to answer and costs little. The "heroes of faith" bear little resemblance to normal heroes. Many of them do not even have their names remembered by the world. Others have known more of the world's disdain and mockery than its respect.

Second, there is another side to the reality of self-denial. From one perspective, demonstrated by all sorts of behavior patterns, it is against all our instincts. Even our physiological reactions in situations of stress and anger are directed toward saving and protecting self. From another perspective, however, we see examples of true denial of self for the sake of someone or something else all the time. They are a large feature of parenthood; all of us know examples of parents who have set aside many of their own desires and needs for the sake of their children's well-being, of mothers who have set aside their own possibilities, ambitions, and enjoyments in the care of sick or disabled children. The list of persons who have given up their lives to save others or in defense of family and country is a long one. Bonhoeffer's words about the cost of discipleship, his famous declaration, "When Christ calls a man, he bids him come and die," were certainly not hollow words as he gave his own life in response to the call of Christ and against the evil and tyranny of Hitler's fanaticism. So it is incumbent upon us in the proclamation of this text to recognize that there is also something within us that can and does respond to a call to set self aside.

Third, all of the examples above suggest that we do not tend to set aside or deny ourselves in response to a moral principle calling us to do so but in response to some one or some thing, a cause to which we give ourselves. That is what self-denial is about in general and in Jesus words: "*If any one would come after me*," let that one deny self and take up the cross. It is in commitment to Christ and Christ's way that we are called *and able* to set aside our ego, our self-instincts. In the cause of Christ and those enterprises in this world that most clearly reflect, embody, and carry out that cause, the giving up of self is a true possibility for discipleship.

Fourth, such a way of thinking and living is finally in some sense self-enhancing, or, in Jesus' words, a way to find self and life. That too is a reality of human experience to which many can bear testimony even when the rest of the world has thought that life was given up without any profit. As he was being taken away to be hanged at Flossenburg, Bonhoeffer turned to his fellow prisoners. "This is the end," he said. "For me the beginning of life." In T. S. Eliot's *The Cocktail Party*, a group of Celia Coplestone's friends are shocked and dismayed when they hear of her torture and death during an insurrection and while she was nursing natives dying of pestilence at a Christian village in a far-off land. Her doctor, Sir Henry Harcourt Reilly, tells them:

> As for Miss Coplestone, because you think her death was waste,
> You blame yourselves, and because you blame yourselves,
> You think her life was wasted. It was triumphant.[9]

OLD TESTAMENT: JEREMIAH 15:15–21

What then of Jeremiah's anguished words of complaint to God? How, if at all, does he fit in this call to transformation and denial of self in response to God?

The answer to those questions is not hard to find. For Jeremiah is specifically and clearly an example of one who responded to the call of God (Jeremiah 1) and also an illustration of what that response can require. His words in chapter 15 are an outcry to God about the ostracism, the reproach, and the pain he has borne because he has taken up the call of God (v. 16) and a plea to God to do something to help him in his plight.

Jesus' words about self-denial and taking up the cross identify such a way as characteristic of disciples *in general.* Jeremiah's words sharpen our awareness of the pain that may come to those who go that way. Paul in Romans 11 speaks twice of "grace given" to each of us. Jeremiah is a demonstration of "grace given" and a reminder that however real and durable it may be, that grace is neither cheap nor easy. In other words, Jeremiah's lament set in the context of his life experience—isolation, plots against his life, imprisonment, exile—gives concreteness to what Jesus is talking about in taking up the cross.

What is also important, however, is that Jesus' words and the response of God to Jeremiah (15:19–20) offer an assurance that the disciple does not walk the way of discipleship, the way of the cross, alone. Such assurance is found first of all in the realization that Jesus has walked that way before us, so whatever fate may overtake us, it is not unknown to God. Because Jesus has called us and set us on a way that is not strange to him, then it may be possible for us to walk the way also. These words from Scripture are given to us not only to remind us of what the call of God means but also to reassure us of the possibility of our living that out and enduring in the face of terrible demand or great perversity. The other note of assurance here is in God's words to Jeremiah, "I am with you," "I will deliver"; realities sealed in Jesus' promise, "Lo, I am with you always," and in God's act in Jesus Christ to be with us ("Emmanu-el") and to save ("Jesus").

The Sixteenth Sunday After Pentecost

Lutheran	Roman Catholic	Episcopal	Pres/UCC/Chr	Meth/COCU
Ezek. 33:7–9	Ezek. 33:7–9	Ezek 33:(1–6), 7–11	Ezek. 33:7–9	Ezek. 33:1–11
Rom. 13:1–10	Rom. 13:8–10	Rom. 12:9–21	Rom. 13:8–10	Rom. 12:9—13:10
Matt. 18:15–20	Matt. 18:15–20	Matt: 18:15–20	Matt. 18:15–20	Matt. 18:15–20

Issues of authority in religious and civil life as well as issues of our relationship to other members of the community are the central concerns of the lessons for this Sunday. What is our responsibility to brothers and sisters is the faith whose conduct is questionable or immoral, especially if their actions have been directed toward us? What is our proper attitude in word and deed toward civil government? Does obedience to God affect our obedience to law and government? If so, how? These are not easy questions to answer, particularly when we get down to specifics. Christians, however, cannot avoid these issues in their daily life. Paul and Matthew both offer instruction for the Christian community, which from its earliest days until now has had to wrestle with these matters.

EPISTLE: ROMANS 13:1–10

This classic New Testament text on the Christian's responsibility to the state is a forthright claim that Christians are to be loyal and subject to those governing authorities under whom they live. It is important to remember from the start that Paul's teaching on this subject is not a sudden shift from his words in chapter 12 about life in the Christian community. In this passage Paul moves "from the distinctive notes of the Christian life [chap. 12] to its political repercussions and then back again to the special Christian way."[10] But the words about the "political repercussions" are not a side note or a digression. They are set in a context—Paul's words about living together in the Christian fellowship in Romans 12 and 13:7—15:13—that makes the political sphere a significant dimension of the Christian life and part of the order of Christian community. While Paul clearly distinguishes between the church and the civil order, his words resist a sharp separation of the spiritual or religious life from the political, much less any division into two realms. A necessary and appropriate part of the Christian life is responsibility to and involvement in the political order. Those whose citizenship is in heaven (Phil. 3:20) do not give up their citizenship on earth or separate the two from each other. One expression of the Christian life and Christian community—and obviously a significant one to Paul—is participation in the life of the political community.

Subjection to the civil authorities, which, of course, is not the same thing as unthinking or unquestioning obedience, is, therefore, a part of *our living under the rule of God and the lordship of Jesus Christ*. Paul is explicit and clear that civil government is instituted by God (v. 1), the ruling authorities are servants of God (a point that is made three times in vv. 4, 6), and God will respond to our conduct in civil and political matters (v. 5). In some fashion the secular governments carry out God's rule, and as citizens of the kingdom we acknowledge and conform to that rule. They do not stand outside the sphere of God's rule, and they are answerable to God whether they know it or not.

In the opening verse of this chapter there is much that is related to *order*—"authorities," "be subject to," "instituted," "resists." All of this language has to do with God's provision for order, which in biblical terms is one of the primary understandings of what the rule of God is all about—order in the cosmos, which makes a workable, livable world, and order in society, which also makes things workable and livable. All this about God's order means that anarchy and its near kin are not a part of what Paul is talking about. The civil authority is one of the ways—and a crucial one—by which God provides security for life and the possibilities of its full expression. The identification of the secular ruler as God's servant *for good* means that the order God intends is a good one and rules out tyrannical, oppressive, and unjust governments. A critique of bad governments and resistance to political orders that do not express God's good government is implicit in these verses rather than explicit, but it is clear. Respect—in attitude or practice—for the governing authorities and economic support for them are proper expressions of the Christian life and of the search for the kingdom of God. One does not, therefore, ever lightly rebel or withdraw that respect and support. (Tax dodges and complaining about taxes are specifically in view here. Paul would have little truck with the eager grasp of tax loopholes.) If, however, the civil rulers assert an absolute authority or claim on citizens, usurping the claim of God in the human/Christian conscience, if they are a terror to proper conduct and a supporter of bad, if they by their actions are not servants and ministers of God but enemies of God's way, then resistance to their rule may be a proper Christian act and even a duty for citizens of the kingdom of God.

All that being the way Christians are to relate to and respond to the political rulers and governors of society, what about the rest of its members? How do we relate to them? The text answers that question as Paul returns to an earlier theme—the rule of love. By loving one another, we will have obeyed and carried out the law. Conversely, if we wish to know what is the proper expression of love for the neighbor, seeking only his or her good rather than harm, the law gives us concrete indications. Paul makes that clear as he refers to the commandments prohibiting adultery, killing, stealing, or coveting. Obedience to the civil law also is an expression of love for the neighbor. Such matters as zoning regulations, traffic laws, tax codes, and the like are provisions for manifesting good and inhibiting wrong toward our neighbor. One has only to think of examples such as the laws about noise regulation or drunken driving to see how not only the laws of Scripture but also those of society are intended to be the means whereby we show love toward our neighbor.

GOSPEL: MATTHEW 18:15–20

The concern for how God's order and our love for the neighbor are expressed in the human community is the subject matter of the Gospel text also. One commentator has properly labeled this chapter "The Ordering of the Christian Community," and Karl Barth treats Matt. 18:20, the most familiar verse of this passage, under the rubric "The Order of the Community." That is clearly the concern of Matthew 18: instruction to the community of Christians about how they are to carry out their life and govern themselves.

The particular affairs (*pragmata*, v. 19) of the church's order addressed in this text are reconciliation and discipline. Though we are inclined to view them as opposites, they are not unrelated, as Jesus' teaching indicates. The instruction given here, while it is not the last or only word in every situation (other texts dealing with similar situations are 5:21–26; 18:21–35; 1 Cor. 6:1–6; and Gal. 6:1), offers some true and helpful guidance to members of the community about getting along and working together. Those guidelines include at least the following matters.

First, problems that exist between brothers and sisters in the Christian community are dealt with in a spirit of personal and private reconciliation, a mode of conduct that is consistent with Paul's words about owing nothing except to love one another (Rom. 13:8). It is important to note that the one who is wronged makes the conciliatory overtures. There is to be no fostering of resentment or harboring of grudges. Nor do complaint, trial, or discipline take place when one has committed an offense against another until serious efforts have been made at personal reconciliation, acknowledgment of the offense on the part of one and forgiveness on the part of the other.

Second, discipline within the Christian community arises in the presence of a spirit unwilling to acknowledge offense and seek reconciliation and persistent resistance to the community's judgment and wisdom. That judgment may be expressed in smaller groups or the larger whole but it is an indication that our personal relationships are a part of a larger fellowship. Christians live in community. The church and the common life are the context and matrix for our existence, and all the metaphors for the kingdom are corporate. Discipline is one of the ways by which the people of God orders its life and deals with problems but only after many efforts at reconciliation and counsel.

Third, authority in the church as in the state (Rom. 13:1–7) is derived from God and here belongs not to any one individual but to the community, indeed the community of the local congregation (Matt. 18:18). There is a kind of unresolved but healthy tension between this text and its predecessor in 16:18–19, as the one places God's authority in the hands of the individual faithful leader and the other in the wisdom of the local congregation. Such tension is in fact reflected within and across the various church bodies and traditions, reminding us of the value of both individual leadership and corporate judgment as the church carries out its tasks and seeks the mind of Christ.

Fourth, the most familiar part of this text is found in vv. 19–20. We tend to think of Jesus' words about two or three gathered together in his name as having to do with prayer and worship. And indeed v. 19 does speak of petition to God. The context, however, suggests that it is in the business of the church, its affairs, its dealing with matters of governance, authority, relations in the community, discipline, church boards, and the like that Christ will be present. Even in the smallest groups that come together in the name of Christ to seek and do the will of God, Christ is present and God's wisdom will be given. This does not mean that church bodies cannot make large mistakes and forsake the mind of Christ, but the evidence supporting Christ's promise is far greater in the church's experience than the evidence to the contrary. Every pastor and every congregation knows from experience that these words are true and trustworthy and must not be treated lightly or abused.

OLD TESTAMENT: EZEKIEL 33:7–9

The words of the Lord to Ezekiel placing upon him the task of being a watchman over the Lord's people is an Old Testament witness to some of the themes that are prominent in the Epistle and Gospel. Given such a role, the prophet is *a significant part of the divine provision for order in the human community.* In the face of the human proclivity for disorder and sin, the prophet Ezekiel was called to be a reminder to the people of God's will and way, and the consequence of disobedience. Like the civil authorities, the prophet was appointed or designated by God, and in many respects was a key part of the government of God, the means by which the rule of God was carried out in the human community. The judgments and intentions of God were mediated through the prophet, who also called the people to account and reminded them of God's way of righteousness and justice. So in continuity with the other lessons, the text reminds us of the various divine provisions for ordering the life of the human community that it may not fall into anarchy and chaos and that God's righteousness and justice may be manifest rather than human sin and wickedness.

There is a reinforcement also of the directions suggested by Rom. 13:8–10 and Matt. 18:15–17. That is in terms of the *prophet's responsibility for the welfare and fate of others.* Like the Christian who manifests love even, if not especially, toward the enemy and the brother or sister who goes in reconciliation to deal with one who has offended, the prophet is sent to "the wicked," those who have not lived by God's instruction. There is a sense of responsibility and accountability explicitly indicated here. The renewal of human community depends upon the prophet's word of warning.

The text—like the others for this Sunday—at its basic level has to do with *pastoral care.* The warning of the prophet is not simply a trumpet blast through the countryside or a sermon addressed to the community of Israel. The warning is to be given to each individual. It is not simply a general word to the people but an encounter with individual members of the congregation that is meant to lead them to see the shift of life that is required when one has failed to live according to the Lord's direction. We are accustomed to think of the prophetic task as belonging to the act of preaching and social action. Ezekiel's call turns that task into one of shepherding and pastoral care. Indeed it does so in a very ungentle fashion. The prophet is held accountable for failure to appeal to the individual members, to instruct and warn them about the consequences of their actions. The word of preaching goes forth, but it must be followed by individual attention, especially to those members of the flock who have offended or in some fashion turned away.

In a variety of ways, therefore, we hear in the lessons of this Sunday directions about how the community of faith orders its life, lives in the world, builds relationships, deals with human sin and failure, and carries out discipline. A complex of responsibilities is uncovered involving civil authorities, ministers, church officers, and members of the congregation. The law of love controls all but does not negate the need for discipline in the community or subjection to those who under God's rule govern and instruct us.

The Seventeenth Sunday After Pentecost

Lutheran	Roman Catholic	Episcopal	Pres/UCC/Chr	Meth/COCU
Gen. 50:15–21	Sir. 27:30—28:7	Sir. 27:30—28:7	Gen. 4:13–16	Gen. 50:15–21 or Sir. 27:30—28:7
Rom. 14:5–9	Rom. 14:7–9	Rom. 14:5–12	Rom. 14:5–9	Rom. 14:5–12
Matt. 18:21–35	Matt. 18:21–35	Matt. 18:21–35	Matt. 18:21–35	Matt. 18:21–35

As the season of Pentecost leads us into extended reflection on the life, death, and resurrection of Jesus and the meaning of God's work in Christ for our individual life and our life together, we come on this Sunday to the question of human sinfulness and how that is dealt with, both by God and within the community. This subject was once uppermost in the preaching of the church, and in some places and preaching, of course, it still is. But increasingly that is less the case, particularly in the mainline denominations of this country. Many of us find that we are repulsed by a lot of talk about sin. We dislike it and feel that we are browbeaten by a lot of focus upon sin in preaching and liturgy.

There are a variety of reasons for this. In part, such an uneasiness or dislike of sin is due to the middle- and upper-class ethos to which we subscribe. In that context we see ourselves as seeking to live *the* good life, which includes *a* good life, and we genuinely do not see ourselves as constantly beset by sin, if sin is, as one confessional document defines it, "any want of conformity unto or transgression of the law of God" (Westminster Shorter Catechism).

We also have come to a broader understanding of human activity that affects our view of sin in two ways. For one thing, some of the sins that in past times have been denounced so vigorously seem now to many persons trivial or not even morally questionable, for example, card playing, dancing, and even such things as drinking, gambling, profanity, and some kinds of sexual activity that have been regarded traditionally as sinful. Further, we know that much of our behavior is affected by psychological, hereditary, and environmental factors that are not easily controlled by the will to do good. What we have often in the past called sin and wickedness can be seen in some instances now to look more like sickness and the pathological, in need of therapy rather than moral condemnation.

Our difficulty with the notion of sin is also created by the fact that many of us already carry such a heavy load of guilt about ourselves and our life that for the church and its preaching to focus heavily upon that is simply to increase an already intolerable burden.

Nevertheless, to ignore this universal dimension of our experience has its negative effects and ultimately becomes impossible. To try to do so will find us ignoring, covering over, suppressing, or failing to come to terms with the moral dimension of our lives, with the various pulls within us toward self-centeredness and self-idolatry or even neglect of self or others. We may find also that some maladies of the soul are not subject to the usual therapies of even the best doctors, psychiatrists, analysts, or psychologists. The burden of guilt weighs upon us like Christian's burden in *Pilgrim's Progress* and nothing seems to take it off.

This reality of sin and guilt, whatever shape it may take, is experienced in relationship to both those other people whose lives we touch and the God who undergirds our lives and shapes the destinies of all of us. The Gospel and Old Testament texts that are before us declare, as do many other words of Scripture, that our sins toward one another and God can be and have been dealt with, that God is present in and through our individual lives and our common history to deal with the offenses and wrongs that we have committed.

GOSPEL: MATTHEW 18:21–35

The basic way in which God deals with human sin is indicated in this parable told by Jesus as a lesson to Peter. Our sins are overcome and the burden of guilt is taken away by God's great forgiveness and the wave of forgiveness that it sets forth in the community of faith. The parable speaks of a master who forgives a servant's debt that is so great it could hardly be paid with all the wages of a lifetime of hard labor. The story is a pointer first of all to the extravagant forgiveness of God that has released us from the weight of those many "debts" or offenses that characterize our life in this world. That freeing and forgiving love was demonstrated and achieved in the life and ministry and the death and resurrection of Jesus Christ. Then and now, those touched by him in any way have found a release, no matter how great the burden of guilt. The Bible speaks this word over and over again. The psalmist cries out of the depths, "If thou shouldst mark iniquities, Lord, who could stand? But there is forgiveness with thee" (Ps. 130:3–4). A rich biblical imagery speaks of this way of God's dealing with our offenses, our failures, by passing over them, removing them, covering over them, blotting them out. All of those words are a way of declaring the good news that in the most ultimate sense those sins are not held against us, that the slate is always being wiped clean. In that reality we find our deepest sense of release.

Such abundant forgiveness on God's part is meant also to initiate a correspondingly extravagant forgiveness on our part. Both the parable and Jesus' words indicate that the community of faith is to express such forgiveness freely and continually, over and over, without ceasing. No matter how much we do that, it will never match the greatness of God's forgiving love toward us. But as it expresses and carries on that same way, the community will experience reconciliation and healing, and the barriers, the hurt, the guilt that separate us from one another can be removed to be replaced by harmony, love, and a capacity to live and work together.

OLD TESTAMENT: GENESIS 50:15–21

The story of Joseph also tells us about how God can or may deal with our human offenses, but in a somewhat different manner than Jesus' word of forgiveness. This text, which comes at the conclusion of that story, can have little meaning apart from familiarity with all that leads up to it—the brother's offense against Joseph and the complex chain of events that brings them face to face many years later under a wholly new set of circumstances. Any preaching of this text, therefore, will need in some fashion to bring the congregation to the point where the text in Genesis 50 picks up and we find out now in these verses what the long story of Joseph is really about.

The death of their father, Jacob, arouses in the minds and hearts of the brothers the fear: Now that Daddy is dead Joseph may finally pay us back for the wrong we did to him years ago. So they go to him and bow before him proclaiming that they will be his servants and asking him not to turn their sin against him *back against them* but *to forgive* their jealous and harmful actions.

Joseph's response is an interesting one. He sees in the way they approach him the fact that they think the question of how their offense will be dealt with is entirely in his hands. The whole manner of the brothers' approach to Joseph indicates they perceive him as in the place of God when he knows that is not so. What the brothers do not realize is that it is not up to Joseph to deal with their sin, for God has already done so. It has been dealt with not so much by forgiveness as by *the providence of God*. The *brothers* intended *harm* and did it. That was part of the reality of Joseph's life and he suffered because of it. Yet somehow in the mystery of God's purpose, *God* was intending something *good* and did it. And that too was a part of the reality of Joseph's life. How these two things—the brothers' harm and God's good—can all be a part of the same act the story does not say. There is indeed a mystery here that we cannot penetrate too easily, and the story does not encourage us to try to explain the ins and outs of God's providence or assume in an overly simple way that God always turns human sin into good. The Bible does not tell us that. But here it does tell us a very important story about the conflicts among some brothers that result in the brothers trying to do in one of their number. That is wrong; there is no way of getting around it. But their story is part of a much larger story of God's care for his people, in which the brothers' offense becomes a part of the way in which God provides for the larger community. Joseph, as a matter of fact, does not actually forgive the brothers' sin against him; nor does he, as they feared, turn it back on them in revenge now that he has power. Rather he perceives that God has dealt with it in his providence and Joseph's task now is neither to forgive nor avenge, but *to provide*, to be the instrument of God's good purpose that overcomes and subsumes the human wrong. Thus is the sin overcome and the guilt and fear done away.

EPISTLE: ROMANS 14:5–9

Paul's instruction about different ways of observing the Christian life picks up a different theme from the one we have been dealing with in the Old Testament lesson and the Gospel. It does continue to deal with matters of order, reconciliation, and harmony in the Christian community, which are basic concerns of these Pentecost lessons as they help us think about how to live the Christian life and the common life.

The words of this text are an encouragement to expansiveness, inclusiveness, and pluralism within the Christian community. They are set against efforts at narrow definition of what is Christian activity and the consequent self-righteousness that accompanies such restricting approaches. Paul's words are a constant pressure on us to keep open the community's understanding of what is an appropriate response to God's grace in the manner of one's life. There seems to be a kind of centripetal force at work in the church's corporate life to close in and force a particular profile or understanding of the Christian life. Paul presses us always toward a more centrifugal, open, accepting profile that recognizes differences and finds them acceptable without judging one person's mode of response, one individual's way of living the Christian life, more acceptable, more Christian than another. People may observe the Sabbath or the Lord's day in different ways. They may have different understandings of what activities (eating, drinking, playing, working) are appropriate for their Christian life. That is OK. It is all right to view those matters more restrictively for oneself or more openly. But my definition is not to be imposed upon you, says Paul.

Only one criterion is set forth as a guide to what is acceptable, and it is the crucial one, preventing Paul's instruction from being an anything goes policy for the sake of harmony and avoiding self-righteousness. The one governing reality is that everything be done to honor God. If that is the truly controlling motive then in that context all is permissible. Or, at the least, very different if not opposite modes of life or piety are permissible. We live to or for the Lord all our lives and in our death. Whatever actions are done as an expression of our devotion to the Lord are good and proper and not to be judged by others. Nor are we to judge the ways of others so motivated. In that context anything goes because only one thing matters. That is the true meaning of freedom in the Christian community. It is also the way to harmony, unity, and humility in our life together.

The Eighteenth Sunday After Pentecost

Lutheran	Roman Catholic	Episcopal	Pres/UCC/Chr	Meth/COCU
Isa. 55:6–9	Isa. 55:6–9	Jon. 3:10—4:11	Isa. 55:6–11	Isa. 55:6–11
Phil. 1:1–5 (6–11), 19–27	Phil. 1:20c–24, 27a	Phil. 1:21–27	Phil. 1:21–27	Phil. 1:1–11, 19–27
Matt. 20:1–16	Matt. 20:1–16	Matt. 20:1–16	Matt. 20:1–16	Matt. 20:1–16

OLD TESTAMENT: ISAIAH 55:6–11
GOSPEL: MATTHEW 20:1–16

The Old Testament lesson and the Gospel are very theological in that their primary focus is on God and God's ways in the world. Proclamation of these texts should serve their theological intent by pointing the congregation to the one who is the ground of all our being and the object of our ultimate devotion and trust, leading the hearers to think with heart and mind about the Lord of life. Such preaching can aid faith as it both seeks understanding and builds trust. It also will have some things to say about how Christian faith responds to God in attitude and conduct.

The purposes and ways of God are the chief subject matter of the texts. While those plans are not decoded for us, we learn some things of importance for Christian faith and life. The first of those lessons is that the plans and ways of God are not the same as human plans. At one level that fact is obvious, but the Bible insists on scoring the point again and again because of our propensity for projecting our own ways and thoughts onto God. That happens within Scripture and constantly in human life. Such projection is not altogether avoidable or even wrong. But we always need to remember that it is seeing "through a glass darkly," a very finite and limited understanding. The point of Isa. 55:8–9 is not just that the Lord's ways are different or opposite but that they utterly transcend our ways in the sense that a mountain so transcends a speck of dust that one cannot remotely conceive of the former from the latter. Contemporary understanding of the nature of the universe has made the comparison in these verses even stronger. Our awareness of the vastness of the universe relative to our place in it is a helpful simile for thinking of the transcendence, the majesty, and the mystery of God.

A second word about God's ways that is consistent with the first but comes especially from the Gospel text is that God does the unexpected, that which is startling and indeed often counter to human expectations. Equal pay for equal work is a universal dictum. But *equal* pay for *unequal* work! That is what is the parable says about the ways of God. One interpreter has called this the Parable of the Eccentric Employer. Such a title points us at least to the surprising character of God's ways and thoughts when viewed from a human perspective.

Both Old Testament and Gospel texts indicate, however, that the transcendent and unexpected purposes of God are good news for us rather than bad news. In Isaiah 55 the transcendent and unexpected ways of God are demonstrated in God's abundant pardon (v. 7b). The mercy of God exceeds human manifestations of reward and retribution as the heavens are higher than the earth. In other words it is the greatness of the Lord's loving mercy that exemplifies God's transcendent majesty. The wholly otherness of God is a source of awe, of fear and trembling, but not of comfort—until it is seen to have its primary manifestation in God's grace toward the creation. In like manner Matthew's parable says that what is surprising about God is a righteousness and goodness not tied to just desserts. The human grumbling in the story comes not because some do not receive a good reward appropriate to their labors but because some receive a good reward far transcending the amount of work they contributed. At the human level, that is indeed a story of eccentricity. But as a glimpse of the ways of God, it is most surely a surprising word of grace. In communicating in startling fashion the fact that "God gives infinitely more than a just wage"[11] the Gospel parable repeats the good news declared by the Old Testament prophet.

Especially in the Old Testament lesson we hear the further good news that the plans and ways of God have an effecting power for good and so can be trusted (Isa. 55:10–11). Both points need to be emphasized. The extended imagery of the rain and snow watering the earth and causing seed to sprout, which eventually becomes bread to eat, is a way of underscoring the capacity of God's word to bring things about and more particularly to bring about good ends, the blessing of God. What is announced by the prophet is carried out and brought to completion by the power of God. That means further that God's word can be depended upon. As David Livingston once said, rather quaintly but pointedly, in regard to Jesus' promise to be with his followers always, "It is the word of a gentleman, and there's an end to it." He knew that the word of the Lord could be trusted. As one assumes the turn of the seasons, the capacity of water to quench thirst, the pull of gravity, or the love of a spouse, so one can count upon God's purposes to succeed, even when there are many signs to the contrary. The human instinct to trust has its deepest ground and clearest confirmation in the surety of God's word and promise.

Finally, these texts make us aware that the theological realities described above have implications for human conduct. Those implications are many, of course, but here two are presented. The abundant mercy of God is there to call us back from thoughts and acts, attitudes and conduct that are wicked and unrighteous, that betray or corrupt our devotion to God and our love for the neighbor. Matthew's parable of the eccentric employer also has its point. It is a word against a grudging, grumbling attitude and particularly on the part of the strong against the weak, the old-timer against the newcomer, the faithful against the sometime Christian. The surprising love of God means that human standards for accepting one another are not fully adequate. It is the generous goodness of the Lord that becomes the model for our acceptance of others in the community, however much or little we think they may have earned or deserved it.

EPISTLE: PHILIPPIANS 1:1–11, 19–27

Joy and affection may seem a strange matrix for the development of theology and ethics, but Paul's letter expresses convictions about Christian faith and life in just such personal dimensions and human relationships. In the first chapter Paul speaks about what has happened to him and how he cares about the Philippian church. If one listens carefully to how he speaks and notes the frequent references to grace, prayer, and joy or the expansive and frequent use of "all," one will hear the tone of Paul's words and perceive the most important clue to the nature of Christian community that the book gives us. That is its character as a *fellowship of joy.*

This does not mean that Christian community is simply a matter of continually happy faces. Human existence will bring sorrow and tears, disappointment, frustration, and anger in the church no less than outside. Indeed there are clear signs in this letter of problems in the Philippian church. The joy that Paul conveys when he speaks about Christian community is more complex and exists in and through all these other experiences. Its components include at least a number of things that may be identified from Paul's words.

One of these elements creating a fellowship of joy is the sense of a common devotion to the service of Christ and the work of the church. This is what Paul means by partnership in the gospel—a shared participation in the communication of the gospel and the building up of the kingdom of God. The Philippians' work in the proclamation of the gospel and the nurturing of their church—teaching, service, administration, and the like—and Paul's preaching, imprisonment, and trials bind them together in a more than human fellowship that elicits from Paul expressions of thanksgiving and joy (cf. 1:18). When he speaks of the Philippians as "partakers with me of grace, both in my imprisonment and in the defense and confirmation of the gospel," he reiterates their fellowship with him, their belonging together in a community that is grace-full even when its members are undergoing imprisonment and trial.

Such a fellowship is created and held together by shared lives that are devoted fully to Christ and the glory of God. Paul alludes to this several times. It is the theme of his discussion of the tension he feels between choosing life or choosing death (vv. 19–26). Either way, life or death, he is with Christ. It is the same conviction he expressed to the Christians at Rome: "If we live, we live to the Lord, and if we die, we die to the Lord; so then whether we live or whether we die, we are the Lord's" (Rom. 14:8). Elsewhere in his prayer for the Philippian Christians, Paul sees all of their conduct, their attitudes, their understanding as set "to the glory and praise of God" (1:9–11). The somewhat more austere divines of the Westminster Assembly understood well what Paul was getting at when they stated that our chief end in life is "to glorify God and enjoy him forever" (Westminster Shorter Catechism).

It is of course not necessarily easy for a community to live its life fully to Christ and the praise of God. There are clear indications that Paul is trying to help this band of Christians pull that off better than they have in the past. Much of the rest of the Epistle is aimed in that direction. In this chapter Paul suggests at least two things that serve to nurture such a directed life. One of these is *prayer.* It is clear that Paul holds this Christian community constantly in prayer, especially for the quality and character of their life in Christ (1:9–11). In like manner he expects their prayers to undergird him in prison that he may not be ashamed and that "Christ may be honored in my body" (1:19–20). Christian community and discipleship are not brought about simply by dint of our own acts and achievements. Prayer for the support of Christ for one another is an essential ingredient.

The other counsel Paul offers to help Christians keep their lives directed toward the glory of God is an encouragement to focus on the things that really matter rather than on peripheral concerns ("so that you may approve what is excellent," 1:10). In contemporary parlance we speak of this as "centering" one's life, letting go of a lot of activities, involvements, and responsibilities that sap one's time and energies to concentrate on what one cares most about. Paul speaks—and prays—on behalf of such centering. That is not, of course, for him a centering on self, or on what one seems to need or desire most. Such centering goes on very commonly and psychologically may be very healthy. The excellent things that Paul wants to have held in focus are those matters that build up the fellowship and nurture life together in Christ. The rest of his letter tells us what some of those excellent things are.

The Nineteenth Sunday After Pentecost

Lutheran	Roman Catholic	Episcopal	Pres/UCC/Chr	Meth/COCU
Ezek. 18:1–4, 25–32	Ezek. 18:25–28	Ezek. 18:1–4, 25–32	Ezek. 18:25–29	Ezek. 18:1–4, 25–32
Phil. 2:1–5 (6–11)	Phil. 2:1–11 or Phil. 2:1–5	Phil. 2:1–13	Phil. 2:1–11	Phil. 2:1–13
Matt. 21:28–32	Matt. 21:28–32	Matt. 21:28–32	Matt. 21:28–32	Matt. 21:28–32

In their book *Habits of the Heart,* Robert Bellah and his coauthors address what they see as the major issue in American life—individualism. They see it in some forms as a central feature of the biblical and republican tradition out of which this society was born but in other forms as having a destructive side that can be cancerous in American society. Their study of individualism and commitment in relation to love and marriage, family, religion, and civic responsibility can be a helpful background for thinking about the texts for this Sunday. From various angles they deal with individual responsibility and commitment in relation both to God and to other members of the community. Their cutting edge touches facets of our life in the Christian fellowship and in the larger society.

OLD TESTAMENT: EZEKIEL 18:1–4, 25–32

Ezekiel's words deal very directly with the issue of individual responsibility and accountability before God. The word of the Lord he passed on addressed exiles who had experienced the disintegration of their life and society. They handled that reality in part by the point of view expressed in the proverb in v. 2, a proverb quoted critically also in Jer. 31:29. Its point is vivid and clear: We are blamed and punished for the actions and sins of others, in this case previous generations. There is some sense in which one generation shares in the consequences of a previous generation's good or bad actions and an individual's actions have results that can greatly affect other members of the community. But both Ezekiel and Jeremiah bring a divine word declaring that this is not a rule of divine justice and that before God we are morally and finally each one accountable for his or her own actions.

That is first of all an *important word about God*, as v. 25 indicates. It is an insistence on the *justice of God* in dealing with the creation and its creatures. How that is worked out in individual lives and the course of human history is far from clear, and many laments (including those in Scripture) of those who do not see this justice echo through the ages. But this insistent declaration to the exiles is itself a response to such laments (v. 25), asserting the reality of God's justice among the people and the need to live and respond on the basis of that reality. There is a further word here about the ways of the Lord in dealing with people. As so many other tests and stories tell us, *the justice of God is controlled by mercy and compassion*. "Have I any pleasure in the death of the wicked, says the Lord God, and not rather that he should turn from his way and live? . . . For I have no pleasure in the death of anyone, says the Lord God; so turn, and live" (vv. 23, 32). That God is just does not mean that God takes any joy or satisfaction in the negative results of human wickedness. The history of Israel and the Christ event are a demonstration writ large that God's purpose and pleasure (they are the same thing) are that all should live.

The biblical insistence that we are responsible for and judged according to our own actions and not the deeds and acts of others is presumably a welcome word, but it is also a critique of attitudes that are pervasive in our society. For alongside the various forms of individualism, there is a countertendency reflected in an unwillingness or reluctance to assume responsibility or accountability for our actions and circumstances. We all too easily blame our situation on others and what they have done or failed to do to or for us. This tendency is seen, for example, in the great increase of negligence law suits, some of which are well justified while others are manifestly efforts to hold others accountable for our situation. We also readily blame environment, or heredity, or family circumstances for what we ourselves and others do or become. Sometimes we even resort to the claim: The devil made me do it! Ezekiel reminds us that even with the obvious interconnections between ourselves and others and the world around us, there is a moral accountability that each of us must assume to choose, decide, and live the life God wants of us, not sloughing off on others the responsibility for our sinful acts and unpleasant circumstances.

There is a further word from the Lord at the conclusion of the long discussion of individual responsibility and the justice of God in chapter

18. It is an obvious implication of all that has been said. Change your ways; turn away from those attitudes and patterns of behavior that demonstrate faithlessness to God and harm others. Here is the gospel call to repentance in the sure confidence (v. 32) that God desires only good and not ill for us. The proclamation of this word needs to say as clearly as any psychiatrist or analyst, indeed more clearly, that *people can change*, that we are not immutably bound by what we have done or been and what has happened to us in the past. We are called to get a new heart and a new spirit, which means to break from sinful patterns and transform our lives in directions more in tune with the will of God. No word is sounded more clearly in the Bible, but it encounters a modern resistance because we have heard too often that the patterns of our behavior are early set and fixed. The story of the gospel, from Paul and his contemporaries down to the present, is a vivid contradiction to that assumption, whether it is seen in the more dramatic turns of a Paul or a Thomas Merton, or in the countless members of Alcoholics Anonymous who have turned their lives around. All these people have found that change is possible and have known that in their desire and ability to get a new heart and a new spirit, to turn and live, God was at work within them to enable change to take place (cf. Ezek. 36:26–27).

GOSPEL: MATTHEW 21:28–32

Jesus' parable of the two sons is an echo of the word of the Lord in Ezekiel. Once again it is a claim that we are accountable to God for our actions and a call to penitence and true obedience to the will of God. In this context the point is made by a contrast between the obviously sinful, that is, tax collectors and prostitutes (the preacher may want to translate into more appropriate contemporary categories, for example, the slum landlord, the underworld enforcer, or the pimp), who do really turn, repent, get a new heart and a new spirit, and so live as true subjects of the kingdom of God, and between the apparently righteous or just, those of us who manifest religious characteristics but do not in fact seek first the kingdom of God and its righteousness. The parable is thus "a harsh judgment upon those who say 'yes' verbally and intellectually without seeing that the will of God is realized in their lives; at the same time it is an urgent call to such realization".[12] Jesus' refinement on the word of the Lord in Ezekiel is to sharpen up the issue of who are truly the righteous and the wicked. The issue continues to revolve around the change of heart and mind and a reorientation toward the will of God. In both Old Testament and New it has to do with following after the Lord by following the right paths.

EPISTLE: PHILIPPIANS 2:1–13

The Old Testament lesson and the Gospel address the issue of the individual before God. No individuals, however, exist on their own, apart from relation to other persons. It is in this interpersonal and intersocietal context that individualism can turn into a destructive force. There are signs that that happened in the church at Philippi and so Paul felt it necessary to confront and challenge such harmful individualism in his words in the first part of chapter 2 of his Philippian letter. Several things stand out in this challenge.

First, Paul's appeal to his Christian friends to think and act beyond themselves is not set forth as criticism or condemnation but rather as a possibility that arises out of their shared relationship to Christ. Whatever the present reality, Paul knows that within the Christian community there are bonds of love, affection, and compassion that can be the ground for building up harmonious community rather than dissolving into a fragmented individualism. Individualism loses its cancerous power in the midst of a community of persons who care about one another.

Second, the mind-set (see discussion of texts for the Fifteenth Sunday After Pentecost) that Christians are called to create values the worth of other persons and sets the good of others and of the community as equally important as one's own good. That does not mean passivity or self-denigration. It has nothing to do with low self-esteem or self-image in the psychological sense, though it has contributed to such. Paul's sense of self was very strong. But he counted the interests, needs, and problems of others as more important than his own. Conceit, and selfishness, and a sense of self-importance are the seedbed of the individualism that eventually breaks down community.

Third, the model and motivating force of such an orientation away from self-enhancement and toward the good of others is the example of Christ (2:5–11). The one who is the Lord of life for the Christian community is the one who did not hold on to what he had, who took the form of servant rather than Lord, who showed us that in the Christian community the self is emptied rather than enhanced. Against all the tendencies to set our individual wants and needs as the first order of business, the imitation of Christ offers us a better way.

Notes

1. J. Christiaan Beker, *Paul the Apostle* (Philadelphia: Fortress Press, 1980), 363.

2. Frederick Buechner, *Wishful Thinking* (New York: Harper & Row, 1973), 33–34.

3. Paul Achtemeier, *Romans* (Atlanta: John Knox Press, 1985), 148.

4. Buechner, *Wishful Thinking*, 33–34.

5. Eduard Schweizer, *The Good News According to Matthew* (Atlanta: John Knox Press, 1975), 322–23.

6. Karl Barth, *Church Dogmatics* II/2 (Edinburgh: T. & T. Clark, 1957), 285.

7. C. E. B. Cranfield, *Romans: A Shorter Commentary* (Grand Rapids: Wm. B. Eerdmans, 1985), 290–91.

8. T. S. Eliot, "The Rock," in *The Complete Poems and Plays 1909–1950* (New York: Harcourt Brace Jovanovich, 1971), 101.

9. *The Cocktail Party*, in ibid., 385.

10. Barth, *Church Dogmatics*, 723.

11. Schweizer, *The Good News According to Matthew*, 393.

12. Ibid., 412.